First World War
and Army of Occupation
War Diary
France, Belgium and Germany

18 DIVISION
Divisional Troops
Divisional Trench Mortar Batteries
31 December 1915 - 31 January 1918

WO95/2026/1

The Naval & Military Press Ltd
www.nmarchive.com
Published in association with The National Archives

Published by

The Naval & Military Press Ltd

Unit 10 Ridgewood Industrial Park,

Uckfield, East Sussex,

TN22 5QE England

Tel: +44 (0) 1825 749494

www.naval-military-press.com

www.nmarchive.com

This diary has been reprinted in facsimile from the original. Any imperfections are inevitably reproduced and the quality may fall short of modern type and cartographic standards.

© **Crown Copyright**
Images reproduced by permission of The National Archives, London, England, 2015.

Contents

Document type	Place/Title	Date From	Date To
Heading	WO95/2026-1		
Heading	18th Division Trench Mortar Batteries Apr 1916-Jan 1919		
Miscellaneous	V18		
Heading	53rd Trench Mortar Battery July 1916		
Heading	War Diary of "V"-18 Heavy Trench Mortar Battery From April 28th 1916 To July 31st 1916 Volume 1		
War Diary	Bray	28/04/1916	28/04/1916
War Diary	Valheureux	29/04/1916	06/05/1916
War Diary	Argoeuves	06/05/1916	19/05/1916
War Diary	Bray	20/05/1916	21/05/1916
War Diary	Billon Wood	22/05/1916	25/06/1916
War Diary	Gun Line	26/06/1916	21/07/1916
War Diary	Camp	22/07/1916	23/07/1916
War Diary	Erondelle	24/07/1916	26/07/1916
War Diary	Longpre	27/07/1916	27/07/1916
War Diary	Eecke	28/07/1916	31/07/1916
Heading	War Diary of V 18 Heavy Trench Mortar Battery From July 1st 1916 To July 31st 1916 (Volume I)		
War Diary		01/07/1916	31/07/1916
Heading	War Diary of V 18 Heavy Trench Mortar Battery From July 1st 1916 To July 31st 1916 (Volume I)		
War Diary	Camp	22/07/1916	23/07/1916
War Diary	Erondelle	24/07/1916	26/07/1916
War Diary	Longpre	27/07/1916	27/07/1916
War Diary	Eecke	28/07/1916	31/07/1916
War Diary	Gun Line	01/07/1916	21/07/1916
War Diary	Camp	22/07/1916	23/07/1916
War Diary	Erondelle	24/07/1916	26/07/1916
War Diary	Longpre	27/07/1916	27/07/1916
War Diary	Eecke	28/07/1916	31/07/1916
War Diary	Gun Line	01/07/1916	21/07/1916
War Diary	Camp	22/07/1916	23/07/1916
War Diary	Erondelle	24/07/1916	26/07/1916
War Diary	Longpre	27/07/1916	27/07/1916
War Diary	Eecke	28/07/1916	31/07/1916
Heading	War Diary of V 18 Heavy French Mortar Battery From Aug 1st 1916 To Aug 31st 1916 (Volume II)		
War Diary	Eecke	01/08/1916	03/08/1916
War Diary	Le Kirlem	04/08/1916	08/08/1916
War Diary	Erquingham	09/08/1916	25/08/1916
War Diary	Le Kirlum	26/08/1916	29/08/1916
War Diary	Doullens	30/08/1916	31/08/1916
Heading	War Diary of V 18 Heavy Trench Mortar Battery R.A. From September 1st 1916 To September 30th 1916 (Volume V)		
War Diary	Albert	01/09/1916	30/09/1916
Heading	War Diary of V 18 Heavy Trench Mortar Battery From Oct 1st 1916 To Oct 31st 1916 (Volume VI)		
War Diary	Albert	01/10/1916	03/10/1916

War Diary	Q30 b 80.30	04/10/1916	05/10/1916
War Diary	Albert	06/10/1916	08/10/1916
War Diary	W 18b 30.70	09/10/1916	31/10/1916
Miscellaneous	To Headquarters R.A. 18th Div	02/10/1916	02/10/1916
Heading	War Diary of V/18 Heavy Trench Mortar Battery From 1st November 1916 To 30th November 1916 (Volume VII)		
War Diary	In Dug Outs At w 18. c 30.70	01/11/1916	30/11/1916
Heading	War Diary of V/18 Heavy Trench Mortar Battery From 1st December 1916 To 31st December 1916 (Volume VI)		
War Diary	Aveluy W. 18.c. 30.70	01/12/1916	03/12/1916
War Diary	Petit Port	04/12/1916	11/12/1916
War Diary	Grandlaviers	12/12/1916	29/12/1916
War Diary	Acheux	30/12/1916	30/12/1916
War Diary	V.12.c.4.5	31/12/1915	31/12/1915
Heading	War Diary of V/18 Heavy Trench Mortar Battery From January 1st 1917 To January 31st 1917 (Volume VII)		
Miscellaneous	To Headquarters R.A. 18th Div	05/02/1917	05/02/1917
War Diary	Aveluy Wood	01/01/1917	31/01/1917
War Diary	Aveluy Wood	18/01/1917	30/01/1917
Heading	War Diary of V/18 Heavy Trench Mortar Battery From 1st February 1917 To 28th February 1917 (Volume VIII)		
War Diary	Aveluy Wood	01/02/1917	28/02/1917
War Diary		01/02/1917	24/02/1917
War Diary		25/02/1917	28/02/1917
Heading	War Diary of V/18 Heavy Trench Mortar Battery From 1st February 1917 To 28th February 1917 (Volume VIII)		
War Diary	Aveluy Wood	01/02/1917	28/02/1917
War Diary		01/02/1917	24/02/1917
War Diary		07/02/1917	28/02/1917
Heading	War Diary of V/18 Heavy Trench Mortar Battery R.A. From March 1st 1917 To March 31st 1917 (Volume IX)		
War Diary	Aveluy Wood	01/03/1917	06/03/1917
War Diary	R 32d 0.8 Dugouts	07/03/1917	08/03/1917
War Diary	Aubigny	09/03/1917	10/03/1917
War Diary	Arras	11/03/1917	31/03/1917
Heading	War Diary of V/18 Heavy Trench Mortar Battery From 1st April 1917 To 30th April 1917 (Volume X)		
War Diary	Arras	01/04/1917	28/04/1917
War Diary	Pernes	29/04/1917	29/04/1917
War Diary	Beaurains	30/04/1917	30/04/1917
Miscellaneous	Programme of Fire by Capt L. Haybittel. Comdg. V/18 Heavy Trench Mortar Battery Appendix VI.	03/04/1917	03/04/1917
Miscellaneous	Alteration to Programme of Fire Appendix V. 2	04/04/1917	04/04/1917
Miscellaneous	Officer i/c MAC Appendix V.3	04/04/1917	04/04/1917
Miscellaneous	Officer i/c LIZZ Appendix V.4	04/04/1917	04/04/1917
Miscellaneous	Officer i/c MAC Appendix V.5.	05/04/1917	05/04/1917
Miscellaneous	Alteration To Programme of Fire Appendix V. 6.	05/04/1917	05/04/1917
Miscellaneous	Alteration To Programme of Fire Appendix V. 7.	06/04/1917	06/04/1917
Miscellaneous	Officer i/c MAC Appendix V.7a	06/04/1917	06/04/1917
Miscellaneous	Alteration To Programme of Fire Appendix V.8	07/04/1917	07/04/1917
Miscellaneous	Officer i/c. LIZZ. Appendix V.9.	08/04/1917	08/04/1917
Miscellaneous	Officer i/c. LIZZ. Appendix V.10	08/04/1917	08/04/1917

Heading	War Diary of V/18 Heavy Trench Mortar Battery From 1st May 1917 To 31st May 1917 (Volume XI)		
War Diary	Beaurains	01/05/1917	31/05/1917
Heading	War Diary of V/18 Heavy Trench Mortar Battery From 1st June 1917 To 30th June 1917 (Volume XII)		
War Diary	Beaurains	01/06/1917	02/06/1917
War Diary	Henin-Sur-Cojeul	03/06/1917	27/06/1917
War Diary	Hendecourt Les-Ransart	28/06/1917	30/06/1917
Heading	War Diary of V/18 Heavy Trench Mortar Battery From 1st July 1917 To 31st July 1917 (Volume XIII)		
War Diary	Hendecourt	01/07/1917	03/07/1917
War Diary	Doullens	04/07/1917	04/07/1917
War Diary	Steenwoorde	05/07/1917	12/07/1917
War Diary	Camp at H.26.d.5.5	13/07/1917	23/07/1917
War Diary	H.26.d.5.5	24/07/1917	31/07/1917
Heading	War Diary of V/18 Heavy Trench Mortar Battery From 1st August 1917 To 31st August 1917 Vol 14.		
War Diary	Camp at H.26.d.5.5	01/08/1917	30/08/1917
War Diary	Ouderzeele	31/08/1917	20/09/1917
War Diary	Serques	20/09/1917	24/09/1917
War Diary	Zeggers-Cappel	25/09/1917	25/09/1917
War Diary	Poperinghe	26/09/1917	28/09/1917
War Diary	Vlamertinghe	29/09/1917	13/10/1917
War Diary	Trois-Tours	16/10/1917	31/10/1917
War Diary	Trois Tours	01/11/1917	30/11/1917
War Diary	Trois Tours	12/11/1917	29/11/1917
Heading	V/18 H.T.M. Battery December 1917		
War Diary	Trois Tours	01/12/1917	12/12/1917
War Diary	Crombeke	13/12/1917	31/12/1917
War Diary			
Heading	War Diary of V/18 Heavy Trench Mortar Batty For January 1918 Vol 19.		
War Diary	Crombeke	01/01/1918	01/01/1918
War Diary	B.9.c.1.4	01/01/1918	17/01/1918
War Diary	B.9.c.1.4	05/01/1918	24/01/1918
War Diary	B.9.c.1.4	05/01/1918	31/01/1918
War Diary	B.9.c.1.4	06/01/1918	29/01/1918
Miscellaneous	W 18		
Heading	War Diary of W/18 Heavy Trench Mortar Battery From 21st May 1916 To 31st May 1916 (Volume I)		
Miscellaneous	The D.A.G. 3rd Echelon		
War Diary	Argoeuves	21/05/1916	31/05/1916
Heading	War Diary of W/18 Heavy Trench Mortar Batty R.A. From June 1st 1916 To June 30th 1916 (Volume II)		
War Diary	Argoeuves	05/06/1916	05/06/1916
War Diary	Picquigny	09/06/1916	09/06/1916
War Diary	Argoeuves	11/06/1916	11/06/1916
War Diary	Billon Wood	11/06/1916	11/06/1916
War Diary	Bray	14/06/1916	30/06/1916
Heading	War Diary of W/18 Heavy Trench Mortar Battery R.A. From July 1st 1916 To July 31st 1916 (Volume III)		
War Diary	Billon Wood Near Bray	01/07/1916	19/07/1916
War Diary	Near Meaulte	19/07/1916	23/07/1916
War Diary	Erondelle	23/07/1916	26/07/1916
War Diary	Pont-Remy	26/07/1916	28/07/1916
War Diary	Eecke	29/07/1916	31/07/1916

War Diary	Eecke	30/07/1916	30/07/1916
Heading	War Diary of W/18 Heavy Trench Mortar Battery R.A. From July 1st 1916 To July 31st 1916 (Volume III)		
War Diary	Billon Wood Near Bray	01/07/1916	18/07/1916
War Diary	Near Meaulte	19/07/1916	23/07/1916
War Diary	Erondelle	23/07/1916	25/07/1916
War Diary	Pont-Remy	26/07/1916	27/07/1916
War Diary	Bailleul	28/07/1916	28/07/1916
War Diary	Eecke	29/07/1916	31/07/1916
War Diary	Eecke	30/07/1916	30/07/1916
Heading	War Diary of W/18 Heavy Trench Mortar Battery R.A. From August 1st 1916 To August 1916 (Volume IV)		
War Diary	Eecke	01/08/1916	03/08/1916
War Diary	Lekirlem	04/08/1916	08/08/1916
War Diary	Erquinghem Lys	09/08/1916	24/08/1916
War Diary	Erquinghem Lys	11/08/1916	25/08/1916
War Diary	Lekirlem	25/08/1916	29/08/1916
War Diary	Doullens	29/08/1916	31/08/1916
Heading	War Diary of W/18 Heavy Trench Mortar Battery R.A. From September 1st 1916 To September 30th 1916 (Volume V)		
War Diary	Albert	01/09/1916	30/09/1916
Heading	War Diary of W/18 Heavy Trench Mortar Battery From October 1st 1916 To October 31st 1916 (Volume VI)		
War Diary	Albert	01/10/1916	09/10/1916
War Diary	Aveluy	09/10/1916	31/10/1916
War Diary	Aveluy	28/10/1916	28/10/1916
Miscellaneous	X18		
Heading	War Diary For November 1916 X/18 M.T.M. Bty		
War Diary	St Pol Albert	00/09/1916	00/09/1916
War Diary	St Pol	18/09/1916	18/09/1916
War Diary	Colincamps	16/09/1916	16/09/1916
War Diary	Albert	17/09/1916	31/10/1916
Heading	War Diary of "X" 18 Trench Mortar Battery From December 1st 1916 To December 31st 1916 (Volume VI)		
War Diary	Petit-Port	17/12/1916	31/12/1916
War Diary	Albert	01/12/1916	03/12/1916
War Diary	Petit Port	04/12/1916	16/12/1916
War Diary	Colincamps	01/11/1916	15/11/1916
War Diary	Bouzincourt	01/01/1917	12/01/1917
War Diary	Authuile Wood	13/01/1917	14/01/1917
War Diary	Authuile	15/01/1917	31/01/1917
War Diary	Authville Wood	01/02/1917	08/03/1917
War Diary	Aubigny	09/03/1917	10/03/1917
War Diary	Arras	11/03/1917	31/03/1917
War Diary	Arras	09/04/1917	24/04/1917
War Diary	Arras	01/04/1917	29/04/1917
War Diary	Beaurains	30/04/1917	18/05/1917
War Diary	St Martin Our-Cojeul	19/05/1917	31/05/1917
War Diary	St Martin Our-Cojeul	01/06/1917	26/06/1917
War Diary	Heudecourt	27/06/1917	30/06/1917
War Diary	Beaurains	17/06/1917	18/06/1917
War Diary	St Martin Our Cojeul	19/06/1917	30/06/1917
War Diary	St Martin Our Cojeul	01/06/1917	26/06/1917
War Diary	Heudecourt	27/06/1917	03/07/1917

War Diary	Doullens	04/07/1917	04/07/1917
War Diary	Steenvoorde	05/07/1917	11/07/1917
War Diary	Dickebusch	12/07/1917	30/08/1917
War Diary	Oudezeele	30/08/1917	20/09/1917
War Diary	Serques	21/09/1917	24/09/1917
War Diary	Zeggers-Cappel	25/09/1917	25/09/1917
War Diary	Poperinghe	26/09/1917	28/09/1917
War Diary	Vlamertinghe	29/09/1917	13/10/1917
War Diary	Trois Tours	14/10/1917	30/11/1917
Heading	X/18 Trench Mortar Battery December 1917		
War Diary	Trois Tours	01/12/1917	13/12/1917
War Diary	Crombeke	14/12/1917	31/12/1917
Heading	X/18 Trench Mortar Battery R.A. January 1918		
War Diary	Crombeke	01/01/1918	01/01/1918
War Diary	Larrey Camp (Elverdinghe)	02/01/1918	31/01/1918
Heading	War Diary of 18th Div War Diary X/18 Trench Mortar Battery, R.A. March 1918.		
War Diary	Remigny	01/03/1918	21/03/1918
War Diary	Villequier Aumont	21/03/1918	31/03/1918
Heading	18th Div. X/18 Trench Mortar Battery, R.A. April 1916		
War Diary	Line of March	01/04/1918	07/04/1918
War Diary	Charny	08/04/1918	09/04/1918
War Diary	Warlus	10/04/1918	10/04/1918
War Diary	Grandsart	11/04/1918	14/04/1918
War Diary	Amiens	15/04/1918	15/04/1918
War Diary	Bours	16/04/1918	29/04/1918
War Diary	St Ouen	30/04/1918	04/05/1918
War Diary	Behencourt	05/05/1918	05/05/1918
War Diary	Line	06/05/1918	29/05/1918
War Diary	Baizieux	30/05/1918	31/05/1918
War Diary	Line	01/06/1918	12/06/1918
War Diary	Baizieux	13/06/1918	15/06/1918
War Diary	Line	16/06/1918	20/06/1918
War Diary	Baizieux	21/06/1918	23/06/1918
War Diary	Line	24/06/1918	28/06/1918
War Diary	Baizieux	29/06/1918	01/07/1918
War Diary	Line	02/07/1918	05/07/1918
War Diary	Baizieux	06/07/1918	13/07/1918
War Diary	Bertricourt	14/07/1918	31/07/1918
Heading	18th Division Artillery X/18 Trench Mortar Battery August 1918		
War Diary	Longpre	01/08/1918	01/08/1918
War Diary	Lahoussoye	02/08/1918	09/08/1918
War Diary	Heilly	10/08/1918	28/08/1918
War Diary	E6c 3.2 (Sheet 62d NE)	29/08/1918	31/08/1918
War Diary	Montauban	01/09/1918	03/09/1918
War Diary	Combles	04/09/1918	05/09/1918
War Diary	Nurlu	06/09/1918	06/09/1918
War Diary	Lieramont	07/09/1917	08/10/1917
War Diary	Lempire	01/10/1918	08/10/1918
War Diary	Serain	10/10/1918	10/10/1918
War Diary	Bertry	11/10/1918	21/10/1918
War Diary	Le Cateau	21/10/1918	28/10/1918
War Diary	Bousies	30/10/1918	06/11/1918
War Diary	Maretz	08/11/1918	31/01/1919
Miscellaneous	Y18		

War Diary	Rollecourt	01/09/1916	08/09/1916
War Diary	Albert	09/09/1916	30/09/1916
Heading	War Diary of Y/18 T.M. Battery For October 1916		
War Diary	In The Field	01/10/1916	31/10/1916
Heading	War Diary For November 1916 Y/18 M.T.M. Bty		
War Diary	In The Field	01/11/1918	30/11/1918
Heading	War Diary of "Y" 18 Trench Mortar Battery From December 1st 1916 To December 31st 1916 (Volume VI)		
War Diary	In The Field	01/12/1916	28/02/1917
Heading	War Diary For March 1917 X.Y. & Z/18 Trench Mortar Batteries Vol 9		
War Diary	In The Field	01/03/1917	31/10/1917
War Diary	Chateau Des Trois Tours	01/11/1917	30/11/1917
War Diary	In The Field	01/12/1917	31/12/1917
War Diary	Crombeke	01/01/1918	01/01/1918
War Diary	B.9.c.14.	01/01/1918	17/01/1918
War Diary	B.9.c.14.	05/01/1918	31/01/1918
War Diary	B.9.c.14.	21/01/1918	29/01/1918
War Diary	Elverdinghe	01/02/1918	02/02/1918
War Diary	Poperinghe	02/02/1918	02/02/1918
War Diary	Amiens	03/02/1918	03/02/1918
War Diary	Vaux-En-Amienois	04/02/1918	19/02/1918
War Diary	Amiens	19/02/1918	20/02/1918
War Diary	Flavy-Le-Martel	21/02/1918	21/02/1918
War Diary	Benay	22/02/1918	28/02/1918
Heading	18th Div. War Diary Y/18 Trench Mortar Battery, R.A. March 1918		
War Diary	Remigny	01/03/1918	21/03/1918
War Diary	Villequier-Aumont	21/03/1918	31/03/1918
Heading	18th Div. Y/18 Trench Mortar Battery, R.A. April 1918		
War Diary	Lieut of March	01/04/1918	07/04/1918
War Diary	Charny	08/04/1918	09/04/1918
War Diary	Warlus	10/04/1918	10/04/1918
War Diary	Grandsart	11/04/1918	14/04/1918
War Diary	Amiens	15/04/1918	15/04/1918
War Diary	Boves	16/04/1918	30/04/1918
War Diary	St. Ouen	01/05/1918	04/05/1918
War Diary	Behencourt	05/05/1918	06/05/1918
War Diary	Line	07/05/1918	28/05/1918
War Diary	Baizieux	29/05/1918	03/06/1918
War Diary	Line	04/06/1918	08/06/1918
War Diary	Baizieux	08/06/1918	11/06/1918
War Diary	Line	12/06/1918	16/06/1918
War Diary	Baizieux	17/06/1918	19/06/1918
War Diary	Line	20/06/1918	24/06/1918
War Diary	Baizieux	25/06/1918	28/06/1918
War Diary	Line	29/06/1918	30/06/1918
Heading	18th Division. Artillery Y/18 Trench Mortar Battery August 1918		
War Diary	Bertricourt	01/08/1918	01/08/1918
War Diary	Heilly	02/08/1918	02/08/1918
War Diary	Line	03/08/1918	08/08/1918
War Diary	Heilly	09/08/1918	28/08/1918
War Diary	E6 c 4.4	29/08/1918	30/08/1918
War Diary	Montauban	31/08/1918	04/09/1918

Type	Location	Start	End
War Diary	Pries Farm	05/09/1918	09/09/1918
War Diary	Lieramont	10/09/1918	05/10/1918
War Diary	Lempire	08/10/1918	08/10/1918
War Diary	Serain	10/08/1918	10/08/1918
War Diary	Bertry	11/08/1918	22/08/1918
War Diary	Le Cateau	23/10/1918	02/11/1918
War Diary	Bousies	03/11/1918	08/11/1918
War Diary	Maretz	09/11/1918	31/01/1919
Heading	Z18		
War Diary	Rollecourt	01/09/1916	08/09/1916
War Diary	Albert	09/09/1916	30/09/1916
Heading	War Diary For October 1916 Z 18th Div. Trench. Mortars Vol 4		
Miscellaneous	18th Divisional Artillery	02/11/1916	02/11/1916
Heading	18th T.M. Batteries (V.X.Y & Z) Vol 8		
War Diary	Albert	30/09/1916	30/09/1916
War Diary	Colincamps	01/10/1916	19/10/1916
War Diary	Hebulirne Edition 2 d.	11/10/1916	31/10/1916
Heading	War Diary For November 1916 Z/18 M.T.M. Bty		
War Diary	Colinchamps	01/11/1916	16/11/1916
War Diary	Albert	17/11/1916	30/11/1916
Heading	War Diary of "Z" 18 Trench Mortar Battery From December 1st 1916 To December 31st 1916 (Volume II)		
War Diary	Albert	01/12/1916	02/12/1916
War Diary	Petit Port	03/12/1916	31/12/1916
War Diary	Bouizincourt	01/01/1917	13/01/1917
War Diary	Authville Wood	14/01/1917	31/01/1917
War Diary	In The Field	01/02/1917	19/02/1917
War Diary	Authville Wood	20/02/1917	21/03/1917
War Diary	Authville Village	22/03/1917	31/03/1917
Heading	War Diary For April 1917 Trench Mortar Batteries V/18 X/18 Y/18 Z/18		
Miscellaneous	Headquarters 18th Divn. Artillery	01/05/1917	01/05/1917
Heading	War Diary For April. 1917 18th Divisional Artillery Vol 10		
War Diary	Hazebrouck	01/04/1917	18/04/1917
War Diary	Hazebrouck	17/04/1917	25/04/1917
War Diary	Oblinghem	26/04/1917	27/04/1917
War Diary	Heuchin	28/04/1917	30/04/1917
Heading	War Diary For May 1917 18th T.M Batteries V/18 X/18 Y/18 Z/18 Vol XI.		
Miscellaneous	18th Divisional Artillery	03/06/1917	03/06/1917
War Diary	Beaurains	01/05/1917	31/05/1917
Heading	18th D.T.M. Btys V/18 X/18 Y/18 Z/18 Vol 12 June 1917		
War Diary	In The Field	01/06/1917	30/06/1917
Miscellaneous	Headquarters 18th Divn Artillery	07/07/1917	07/07/1917
Heading	War Diary For July 1917 18th T.M. Batteries V/18 X/18 Y/18 Z/18 Vol 13		
Miscellaneous	Headquarters 18th Divn Artillery	03/08/1917	03/08/1917
War Diary	Field	01/07/1917	14/07/1917
War Diary	14 7. Zillebeke	14/07/1917	19/07/1917
War Diary	Zillebeke	19/07/1917	31/07/1917
War Diary	Dickebusch.	01/08/1917	31/08/1917
War Diary	Ouderzeele	01/09/1917	20/09/1917

War Diary	Serques	21/09/1917	24/09/1917
War Diary	Poperinghe	25/09/1917	28/09/1917
War Diary	Vilmertingh	29/09/1917	30/09/1917
Heading	18th Division Trench Mortar Batteries. War Diary For Month of October, 1917		
War Diary	Vlamertinghe	01/10/1917	12/10/1917
War Diary	Chateau Des Frois Tours	13/10/1917	13/10/1917
War Diary	Chateau Des Frois Tours	14/10/1917	22/10/1917
War Diary	Chateau Des Trois Tours	23/10/1917	30/11/1917
Heading	Z/18 T.M.B, R.A. December 1917		
War Diary	Chateau Trois Tours	01/12/1917	12/12/1917
War Diary	Crombeke	13/12/1917	31/12/1917
War Diary	Crombeke	01/01/1918	01/01/1918
War Diary	Larry Farm	02/01/1918	07/01/1918
War Diary	Vaux les Amiens	08/01/1918	19/01/1918
War Diary	Larry Farm	20/01/1918	21/01/1918
War Diary	Larry Farm	22/01/1918	31/01/1918

10 05/2026/1

18TH DIVISION

TRENCH MORTAR BATTERIES
APR 1916 - JAN 1919

18TH DIVISION

// 53rd Vol 1

53RD TRENCH MORTAR BATTERY

JULY 1916

V-18
W-18
X-18
Z-18.

XVIII

V. 1. 2. 3
4

Confidential.

War Diary

of

"V" – 18 Heavy Trench Mortar Battery.

From – April 28th. 1916.   to – July 31st 1916.

Volume I.

Army Form C. 2118.

WAR DIARY
INTELLIGENCE SUMMARY
(Erase heading not required.)

Instructions regarding War Diaries and Intelligence Summaries are contained in F.S. Regs., Part II. and the Staff Manual respectively. Title Pages will be prepared in manuscript.

Place	Date	Hour	Summary of Events and Information	Remarks and references to Appendices
BRAY	28th April	9 A.M.	The battery was formed under the command of LT. C.W CRUMPLIN R.F.A. & Lt. W. Sturgh of 69 infantry B.D. + two Subalterns 2nd LT. W.G ALLEN 2nd LT F. ALLEN, four fifths of the other ranks were made up of men drawn from 82nd, 83rd, 84, 85th Brigades + 10th D.A.C. The remainder consisting of R.G.A TERRITORIALS.	
		10 A.M.	The battery left BRAY in Motor-lorries for the 4 ARMY TRENCH MORTAR SCHOOL at VALHEUREUX.	
		4 P.M.	Arrived VALHEUREUX.	
VALHEUREUX	29 April to 30		Battery under instruction on the 9.45" HEAVY TRENCH MORTAR.	

W.G. Crumplin Lt
Commanding V/13 H.T.M Battery
R.F.A.

Army Form C. 2118.

WAR DIARY
INTELLIGENCE SUMMARY
(Erase heading not required.)

Instructions regarding War Diaries and Intelligence Summaries are contained in F. S. Regs., Part II. and the Staff Manual respectively. Title Pages will be prepared in manuscript.

Place	Date	Hour	Summary of Events and Information	Remarks and references to Appendices
VALHEUREUX	1st May 16 to 5th May 16		Battery continued its training at the school.	
VALHEUREUX	6th May	9.AM	Battery left school in Motor Lorries for ARGOEUVES and reported the 18th Division R.H. at watering at 1.P.M.	
ARGOEUVES	"	2.P.M	Battery billeted.	
ARGOEUVES	7th May to 18th May		Battery training	
ARGOEUVES	19th May	9.AM	Battery left in Motor Lorries for BRAY and went into billets.	
BRAY	20th May		Battery in billets	
"	21st May	10.A.M	Battery moved to BILLON WOOD and bivouac	
BILLON WOOD	22nd May to 31st May		Battery digging their gun pits on the N.E. of the village of CARNOY.	

Commanding V/18 H.T. M. Brigade R.H.A

Army Form C. 2118.

WAR DIARY
or
INTELLIGENCE SUMMARY

(Erase heading not required.)

Instructions regarding War Diaries and Intelligence Summaries are contained in F. S. Regs., Part II. and the Staff Manual respectively. Title Pages will be prepared in manuscript.

Place	Date	Hour	Summary of Events and Information	Remarks and references to Appendices
BILLON WOOD	24th June		Battery working on Wire & New Position also dumped gun more ammunition. Shell & ammunition dugouts were made to be depth of about 15ft deep 25ft long about 15ft of head cover.	
BILLON WOOD	25 June		Battery more dumped into the gun pits at N.E. of CARNOY.	
GUN LINE	26 June		One heavy French Mortar arrived (240 m.m.) & was positioned to similar showing French inf.	
GUN LINE	27th June		Seven rounds were fired on the morning FRENCH ammunition & engaging enemy inf. As it did not reach the trench which was 1600 yds. deep began to give way off billet & demoralise the gun no remark to the enemy trenches.	
GUN LINE	28 June		Ten rounds were fired from the 9.45" Mortar onto the 9.45" Position owing to the weather it was not got through. The gun sent to be repaired. A new position 200 yds on front of the new position was selected this was a chasseur old French about 9ft deep. The trench was repaired & the gun was nearly ready for the next day.	
GUN LINE	29 June		Today two rounds were fired from this new position. The gun was found to be very erratic & windage was not stable with the range tables supplied by a strong salient considerable damage was done to the GERMAN Support line and German wagon way road was on dropping near observed.	

2449 Wt. W14957/M90 750,000 1/16 J.B.C. & A. Forms/C.2118/12.

Army Form C. 2118.

WAR DIARY

INTELLIGENCE SUMMARY

(Erase heading not required.)

Instructions regarding War Diaries and Intelligence Summaries are contained in F. S. Regs., Part II. and the Staff Manual respectively. Title Pages will be prepared in manuscript.

Place	Date	Hour	Summary of Events and Information	Remarks and references to Appendices
GUN LINE	30th Jan		Ninety four rounds were fired with good results	

Commander A/15 H.T.M Battery R.A.

Army Form C. 2118.

WAR DIARY
or
INTELLIGENCE SUMMARY

(Erase heading not required.)

Instructions regarding War Diaries and Intelligence Summaries are contained in F. S. Regs., Part II. and the Staff Manual respectively. Title Pages will be prepared in manuscript.

Place	Date	Hour	Summary of Events and Information	Remarks and references to Appendices
GUN.LINE	1st July (Z day)	Between 6.30 P.M. to 7.25 P.M.	The battery fired 12 rounds action over, to our infantry advancing and the enemy retreating. 2/Lt W.G. ALLEN and three others were wounded.	
GUN.LINE	2nd July to 17th July		Battery out of action but remained in their old position. During these dates the battery hostiles firing on wounded & during the nights brought in the following enemy guns:- 4 7.2 German How. 2 77mm Field guns 2 2 Belgium Field guns 1.77cm Trench Mortar (Minenwerfer) and 1 small Belgium field gun. Four other ranks wounded and one killed	
GUN.LINE	18th July		Capt C.W. CROMPLIN RFA assumed command of A/85 th Bde RFA. CAPT. L.M.G. HAYBITTLE LRFA assumed command of the battery.	
GUN LINE	19th July to 20th July		Battery on fatigues	
GUN LINE	21st July	3.30PM	Battery moved to camp at 18 A.D.H.Q on the BRAY-MEAULTE Road	
CAMP	22nd July		Battery at rest. Under orders from VIII Corps RA the gun was handed over complete to V/13 Heavy Trench Mortar Battery AM 3rd division	

2449 Wt. W14957/M90 750,000 1/16 J.B.C. & A. Forms/C.2118/12.

WAR DIARY
or
INTELLIGENCE SUMMARY

(Erase heading not required.)

Army Form C. 2118.

Instructions regarding War Diaries and Intelligence Summaries are contained in F. S. Regs., Part II. and the Staff Manual respectively. Title Pages will be prepared in manuscript.

Place	Date	Hour	Summary of Events and Information	Remarks and references to Appendices
CAMP	23rd July	8.45 P.M	Battery moved by Motor lorries to ERONDELLE arrived there at 4 P.M. and Debouac.	
ERONDELLE	24th July to 25th July		Battery at rest.	
ERONDELLE	26th July	2.30 P.M	Battery marched to LONGPRE and helped R.T.O entraining cavalry Brigades	
LONGPRE	27th July	7.30 P.M	Battery entrained for BAILLEUL and detrained at 5.45 A.M next morning	
EECKE	28th July	10.30 P.M	Battery arrived here on Motor lorries from BAILLEUL and environs.	
EECKE	29th July to 31st July		Battery at rest, doing drills & parades.	

Commanding 1/1 8th Trench Battery
R.H.A

2449 Wt. W14957/M90 750,000 1/16 J.B.C. & A. Forms/C.2118/12.

18 July

r o w T M Ballim

Vol 1

Confidential
War Diary
of
V 18 Heavy Siege Howitzer Brigade
July 1st 1916 to July 31st 1916

(Volume I)

WAR DIARY / INTELLIGENCE SUMMARY

Army Form C. 2118.

53rd T.M.B.

JULY

Place	Date	Hour	Summary of Events and Information	Remarks and references to Appendices
	July 1st	7.20 a.m.	At 7.20 a.m. the battery opened rapid fire on the German front line, and that was maintained just before 7.30 a.m. when the infantry attack was launched. Ammunition had been made for the guns to go forward in pairs and immediately the infantry advanced, 2 guns under 2 Lt Ruckle went forward on the left with the 6 Royal Berkshire Regt. while 2 guns under Lieut Savage supported the 8th Norfolk Regt. The remaining four guns remained in reserve under 2 Lt Osborne and a Sergt in our front line. From the moment of the advance, the emplacements became the forward ammunition dumps. Previous to this, the Brigade had dumped the shells in the Brigade Ammunition store in MONTAUBAN AVENUE, where they were fused, detonated, + cartridged, ↑ Then was used as the advanced dumps which kept the emplacements supplied. All batteries had been divided from the 1st Battalion + these were allotted (largely) to the two guns, there not being to keep the guns supplied, without to the respective guns. There not being to keep the guns supplied, without they might be, built ammunition from the emplacement dumps. This arrangement worked admirably and at no time was any gun	

WAR DIARY or INTELLIGENCE SUMMARY

Army Form C. 2118.

53rd T.M.B.

JULY

Place	Date	Hour	Summary of Events and Information	Remarks and references to Appendices

July 1st — without ammunition.

2nd Lt Osborne was worn out & almost unnerved by the attack & was invalided.

2nd Lt Ruston who went forward on the left & coming to reports them offering (the 6th Berks) did admirable work throughout the day & was especially useful at the POMMIERS line. Part of the battalion was held up momentarily in front of MONTAUBAN ALLEY & 2 Lieut Ruston having blown a suspicious post jumped over the top of the trench and ran slap at a German officer who was one of them and had killed several of the trench. He emptied his revolver at him but unfortunately was killed. The name has been recommended for official recognition.

Lieut. Savage on the right near the Norfolks was wounded with LOOP.

The Norfolks were held up for a considerable time at the base of the LOOP, but were eventually able to go on as the STOKES gun forced the Germans to keep on their to surrender. A considerable party came out and gave themselves up, being unable to withstand

WAR DIARY
or
INTELLIGENCE SUMMARY

Army Form C. 2118.

53rd T.M.B.

JULY

(Erase heading not required.)

Place	Date	Hour	Summary of Events and Information	Remarks and references to Appendices
	July 1st		the demoralising effect of rapid fire, a great many to having been killed or wounded	
	July 2.8		Subsequently the whole 8 guns were at work in MONTAUBAN ALLEY. 10 ammunition waggon brought up – 200 rounds per gun which was put into 8 cases built to receive them. The whole Battery was then up there & remained there for the purpose of repelling any possible counter attack	
	July 8 – 12		Resting at Grovetown Camp, BRAY.	
	July 13.		One gun made an officer were sent to 8 ?? to supply the ?? and to earn repeatedly to the ?? & the ?? live in BERNAFAY WOOD	
	July 19.		Four guns were sent with the 8 ?? Suffolks to help to take LONGUEVAL. Two fired directly down the main street & two fired diagonally into it. These guns assisted in clearing the street. Some snipers first were seen to go up in the air	

WAR DIARY or INTELLIGENCE SUMMARY

33rd T.M.B.

JULY

Army Form C. 2118.

Place	Date	Hour	Summary of Events and Information	Remarks and references to Appendices
LONGUEVAL	July 19		The guns & batteries were then withdrawn to the valley South of LONGUEVAL.	
	July 20		From 7 pm 19th July onwards, ammunition was carried up to LONGUEVAL for the purpose of assisting a brigade of the 3rd Division to take DELVILLE WOOD. The guns were placed in the alley of the wood and were ourselves from the village on a house just N. of the railway line. Rapid fire was delivered from 3.a.m. until 3.30.a.m. when the infantry attack was launched, some 200 rounds being fired from each position. The guns & men were then withdrawn to the valley where they remained until the brigade was relieved on 22nd inst.	
	July 22		Up to Grovetown Camp, BRAY, arriving there at 9 p.m.	
	July 24		Left BRAY for AIRAINES at 10.15 a.m. & arrived there at 6.15 p.m.	

Army Form C. 2118.

WAR DIARY
INTELLIGENCE SUMMARY

53rd T.M.B.

JULY

Place	Date	Hour	Summary of Events and Information	Remarks and references to Appendices
	July 25.		Marched from AIRAINES to LONGPRE, where we entrained at 12.20 p.m. for ARC. We marched from ARC at 8.20 p.m and arrived at LYNDE at 1 a.m. on morning of 26th.	
	July 27.		2nd Lt. J. Græme took over command of the battery from Capt Rogerson	
	July 29		Marched from LYNDE at 4.20 a.m + arrived in GODEWAERSVELDE at 10 a.m.	
	July 31.		2nd Lt Armstrong sent on a Stokes gun course to 2nd Army School at TERDHEGEM. Course from 31st July to 6th August.	

J Græme 2nd Lt
O.C. 53rd T.M.B

18/ KII

Confidential

War Diary

of

V/18 Heavy Trench Mortar Battery

from - July 10th 1916 to July 31st 1916

Copy
(Volume I)

Army Form C. 2118.

WAR DIARY
INTELLIGENCE SUMMARY
(Erase heading not required.)

Instructions regarding War Diaries and Intelligence Summaries are contained in F.S. Regs., Part II. and the Staff Manual respectively. Title Pages will be prepared in manuscript.

Place	Date	Hour	Summary of Events and Information	Remarks and references to Appendices
CAMP	22nd July		Battery at rest. Under orders from XIII Corps R.A. the 9.45 Mortar was handed over complete to V/3 Heavy Trench Mortar Battery R.A. 3rd Division.	###
CAMP	23rd July		Battery moved by motor lorries to ERONDELLE arrived there at 4.P.M and bivouac.	###
ERONDELLE	24th July to 25th July		Battery at rest.	###
ERONDELLE	26th July	2.30 P.M	Battery marched to LONGPRÉ arrived there at 5:30.P.M and hilled and R.T.O entraining Artillery Brigades.	###
LONGPRE	27th July	7.30 P.M	Battery entrained for BAILLEUL and detrained at 5.45 A.M next morning.	###
EECKE	28th July	10.30 P.M	Battery arrived there by motor lorries from BAILLEUL and bivouac.	###
EECKE	29th July to 31st July		Battery at rest doing drills and parades.	###

Margaritta Cent R.F.A
Comdg V/18. H.T.M.B. R.A

WAR DIARY
or
INTELLIGENCE SUMMARY

(Erase heading not required.)

Army Form C. 2118.

Place	Date	Hour	Summary of Events and Information	Remarks and references to Appendices
GUN LINE	1st July (Zday)		Between 6.30AM and 7.25 A.M. the battery fired 12 rounds, the gun was then out of action owing to our infantry advancing and the enemy retiring. 2nd Lt. W. G. ALLEN and three other ranks wounded.	※
GUN LINE	2nd July to 17th July		Battery out of action but remained on their old position. During these dates the Battery helped to bring in wounded and during the nights brought in the following enemy guns:- 4 - 42 German Hows; 26 77m.m. Field guns; 2 - Belgium Field guns; 1 - 17c.m. French Mortar (Minenwerfer), and 1 small Belgium Field gun. Four other ranks wounded.	※
GUN LINE	18th July		CAPT. C.W. CRUMPLIN RFA assumed command of A/65th Bde RFA. CAPT. L.M.G. HAYBITTEL assumed command of the battery.	※
GUN LINE	19th July to 20th July		Battery on fatigues.	※
GUN LINE	21st July	3.30 P.M.	Battery marched to camp at 18th D.A.C on the BRAY-MEAULTE ROAD.	※

Army Form C. 2118.

WAR DIARY
or
INTELLIGENCE SUMMARY
(Erase heading not required.)

Instructions regarding War Diaries and Intelligence Summaries are contained in F. S. Regs., Part II. and the Staff Manual respectively. Title Pages will be prepared in manuscript.

Place	Date	Hour	Summary of Events and Information	Remarks and references to Appendices
GUN LINE	16th July (Z day)		Between 6.30 P.M. to 7.25 P.M. the Battery fired 12 rounds at Stakkingen wer Thes out of action owing to our infantry appearing in the enemy trenches. 2/Lt W.G. ALLEN and Three Others ranks wounded.	##
GUN LINE	16th July To 17th July		Battery out of action but remained in their old position. During this date the Battery helped to bring in wounded & during the nights brought in the following enemy guns:- 4. 4.2 (German How); 2. 77m.m. Field Guns 2. ? Belgium Field guns 1.-17cm Trench Mortar (Minenwerfer) and 1 small Belgium field gun. Few other ranks wounded.	##
GUN LINE	18th July		Capt C.W. CRUMPLIN R.F.A. assumed command of A/85 "Bde" R.F.A. CAPT. L. M.G. HAYBITTLE R.F.A. assumed command of the Battery.	##
GUN LINE	19th July To 20th July		Battery on fatigues.	##
GUN LINE	21st July	3.30 P.M.	Battery marched to Camp at 16 "D" N.C. on the Frony BRAY - MEAULT Road	##
CAMP	22nd July		Battery at rest. Under orders from XIII Corps A.A. the gun was handed over complete to V/3 Heavy Trench Mortar Battery R.A. 3rd Division.	##

Army Form C. 2118.

WAR DIARY
or
INTELLIGENCE SUMMARY

(Erase heading not required.)

Instructions regarding War Diaries and Intelligence Summaries are contained in F. S. Regs., Part II. and the Staff Manual respectively. Title Pages will be prepared in manuscript.

Place	Date	Hour	Summary of Events and Information	Remarks and references to Appendices
CAMP	23rd July	8.45 A.M.	Battery moved by Motor Lorries to ERONDELLE, arrived there at 4 P.M. and rest	
ERONDELLE	24 July to 25 July		Battery at rest.	
ERONDELLE	26 July	2.30 P.M.	Battery marched to LONGPRE and Lefthett R.T.O entraining Artillery Brigade	
LONGPRE	27 July	7.30 P.M.	Battery entrained for BAILLEUL and detrained at 5.15 A.M next morn	
EECKE	28 July	10.30 P.M.	Battery arrived here in Motor lorries from BAILLEUL and bivouac.	
EECKE	29 July to 31 July		Battery at rest, doing drills & parades	

J.Arbuthnot Capt A/H
Commanding V/18 H.T.M. Battery
R.A

Army Form C. 2118.

WAR DIARY
INTELLIGENCE SUMMARY

(Erase heading not required.)

Instructions regarding War Diaries and Intelligence Summaries are contained in F. S. Regs., Part II and the Staff Manual respectively. Title Pages will be prepared in manuscript.

Place	Date	Hour	Summary of Events and Information	Remarks and references to Appendices
GUN LINE	1st July (Zulu)		Between 6.30AM and 7.25AM the battery fired 12 rounds, the guns went then out of action owing to our infantry advancing and the enemy retiring. 2nd Lt. W.G. ALLEN and three other ranks wounded.	
GUN LINE	2nd July to 17th July		Battery out of action but remained on their old position. During these dates the Battery helped to bury men wounded and during the nights brought in the following enemy guns :- 4 - A2 German Hows., 2 - 77mm Field guns, 2 - Belgium Field guns, 2 - 17cm Trench Mortar (Minenwerfer), and 1 small Belgium Field gun. Four other ranks wounded.	
GUN LINE	18 July		CAPT. C.W. CRUMPLIN R.F.A. assumed command of A/55th Bde R.F.A. CAPT. L.M.G. HAYBITTEL assumed command of the battery.	
GUN LINE	19th July to 20th July		Battery on fatigues	
GUN LINE	21st July	3.30 P.M.	Battery marched to camp at 15th D.A.C. on the BRAY-MEAULTE ROAD	

Army Form C. 2118.

WAR DIARY
or
INTELLIGENCE SUMMARY

(Erase heading not required.)

Place	Date	Hour	Summary of Events and Information	Remarks and references to Appendices
CAMP	22nd July		Battery at rest. Under orders from XIII Corps R.A. the 9.45 Mortars was handed over/complete to V/3 Heavy Trench Mortar Battery R.A. 3rd Division.	
CAMP	23rd July		Battery moved by Motor lorries to ERONDELLE arrived there at 4 P.M. and bivouac.	
ERONDELLE	24th July to 25th July		Battery at rest.	
ERONDELLE	26th July	2.30 P.M	Battery marched to LONGPRE arrived there at 5.30 P.M and helped R.T.O. entraining artillery Brigades	
LONGPRE	27th July	7.30 P.M	Battery entrained for BAILLEUL and detrained at 5.45 A.M next morning	
EECKE	28th July	10.30 P.M	Battery arrived here by motor lorries from BAILLEUL and bivouac	
EECKE	29th July to 31st July		Battery at rest doing drills and parade.	

Maynill Cantara
Bom: Hy V/18. H.T.M. B.Y.R.A

Confidential

War Diary

of

N° 18 Heavy Trench Mortar Battery

From:- Aug: 1st 1916. To:- Aug: 31st 1916.

(Volume II)

WAR DIARY
INTELLIGENCE SUMMARY

(Erase heading not required.)

Army Form C. 2118.

Instructions regarding War Diaries and Intelligence Summaries are contained in F. S. Regs., Part II. and the Staff Manual respectively. Title Pages will be prepared in manuscript.

Place	Date	Hour	Summary of Events and Information	Remarks and references to Appendices
EECKE	1st Aug to 2nd Aug		Battery at rest doing drills	A
EECKE	3rd Aug		Battery left here at 9.11PM in Motor lorries for LE KIRLEM arriving there at 11.P.M. and bivouacd.	A
LE KIRLEM	4th Aug to 7th Aug		Battery doing drills and fatigues	A
LE KIRLEM	8th Aug	9.11PM	Battery left here in Motor lorries for ERQUINGHAM arriving there at 10.30 P.M. and billeted	A
ERQUINGHAM	9th Aug		The O.C. reconnoitred for likely position on the 54th INF. BDE front	A
	10th Aug		The O.C. reconnoitred for likely position on the 55th INF. BDE front. Report of position sent to Headquarters R.A. 18th Div. One 9.45 Trench Mortar arrived for the battery	A
ERQUINGHAM	11th Aug		Received orders to prepare position at I15b6070. Left the battery marched and turned billets at LA CHAPLE D'ARMENTIERES. I15C90.70. Commenced work at 11P.M.	A

Army Form C. 2118.

WAR DIARY
or
INTELLIGENCE SUMMARY

(Erase heading not required.)

Instructions regarding War Diaries and Intelligence Summaries are contained in F. S. Regs., Part II. and the Staff Manual respectively. Title Pages will be prepared in manuscript.

Place	Date	Hour	Summary of Events and Information	Remarks and references to Appendices
ERQUIRGHAM	12th Aug to 16th Aug		Battery preparing position at I15C9070 working day and night.	
ERQUIRGHAM	17th Aug		The O.C. interviewed the G.O.C. 54th INF. BDE and decided to alter work on new position at I20D38.72. Working progressing on position at I15C9070.	
ERQUIRGHAM	18th Aug		CAPT. L. HAYBITTEL left for a course on Trench Mortars at 2nd Army School BERTHEN. Work on position at I20D38.72 started. W/18 Heavy Trench Mortar Battery RA supplied men for position at I15C9070.	
ERQUIRGHAM	19th Aug to 20th Aug		Battery working on both positions. Position at I20D38.72 completed work finished on one the night of the 20th.	
ERQUIRGHAM	21st Aug to 23rd Aug		Battery working on position at I15C9070.	
ERQUIRGHAM	24th Aug		Battery relieved by Trench Mortar battery of the 34th DIV. and marched to old billets at ERQUIRGHAM	
ERQUIRGHAM	25th Aug	9 A.M.	Battery left here and marched to LE KIRLUM arrived at 11.30 P.M. and bivouacced.	

Army Form C. 2118.

WAR DIARY
—or—
INTELLIGENCE SUMMARY

(Erase heading not required.)

Place	Date	Hour	Summary of Events and Information	Remarks and references to Appendices
LE KIRLUM	26th Aug		CAPT L HANBITTEA return from French Mortar School. Battery at rest.	
LE KIRLUM	27th Aug to 28th Aug		Battery at rest.	
LE KIRLUM	29th Aug	9 A.M.	Battery marched to BAILLEUL entrained at 1.P.M arrived and detrained at DOULLENS 7.30 P.M Bivouac at Doullens for the night.	
DOULLENS	30th Aug		Battery billeted here	
DOULLENS	31st Aug	3.30	Battery left here in photo lorries for ALBERT arriving there at 7 P.M and billeted in the RUE de BAPAUME.	

Hayworth Capt. QFM.

Commanding 1/18 H.T. 1st Battery RFA

Confidential

War Diary of

N° 18 Heavy Trench Mortar Battery, R.A.

from September 1st 1916 to September 30th 1916

(Volume V.)

Army Form C. 2118.

WAR DIARY
INTELLIGENCE SUMMARY
(Erase heading not required.)

Instructions regarding War Diaries and Intelligence Summaries are contained in F. S. Regs., Part II. and the Staff Manual respectively. Title Pages will be prepared in manuscript.

Place	Date	Hour	Summary of Events and Information	Remarks and references to Appendices
ALBERT	1st Sept to 10th Sept		Battery at rest doing permanents.	A
ALBERT.	11th Sept to 19th		Battery was engaged in digging gun positions for 18th Div. Field Batteries. Headquarters of battery remaining at ALBERT.	A
ALBERT	20th to 23rd		Battery at rest. Training	A
ALBERT	24th to 28th		Battery was engaged in digging gun positions for 18 Div. Field Batteries. Headquarters of battery remaining at ALBERT.	A
ALBERT	29th to 30th		Battery at rest. Training	A

Hayhittle Capt RFA
Commanding V/18 H.T.M. Battery
R.A.

Confidential

War Diary
of

V 18 Heavy Trench Mortar Battery

From :- Oct. 1st 1916 to Oct. 31st 1916

(Volume VI)

WAR DIARY
INTELLIGENCE SUMMARY

(Erase heading not required.)

Army Form C. 2118

Place	Date	Hour	Summary of Events and Information	Remarks and references to Appendices
Albert	1st		Battery supplied men to 82nd & 83rd Brigs R.F.A. to help dig Gun Positions.	#
Albert	2nd		The Battery ordered to relieve 49th Div. Heavy Trench Mortar Batteries in THIEPVAL WOOD. 4 positions taken over only one Gun in action	#
"		4.15 pm	Report on positions sent to Headquarters R.A.	(1)
"		5 pm	One Officer and 30 other ranks returned w/ 49 Heavy Trench Mortar Battery at Q.24.c.80.50	
Albert	3rd	2.30 am	Urgent orders received from Headquarters R.A. that position at Q.30.B.15.70 was to be altered to enable the Gun to shoot on NW corner of SCHWABEN REDOUBT by the 4th inst.	
		11.45 am	Batt'y Headquarters established at Q.30.c.80.30 in dug out. Work commenced on position	
		4.30 pm	Enemy heavily shelled position for two hours & stopped the work. Position badly knocked about as the result of the shelling.	

WAR DIARY
or
INTELLIGENCE SUMMARY

Army Form C. 2118

Place	Date	Hour	Summary of Events and Information	Remarks and references to Appendices
Albert	3rd	6.30 pm	Re saw of shelling reported to Headquarters R.A. Orders again to work on position the next morning	#
Q.30.b 80.30	4th	6am to 11-30	Working on position as ordered.	
		11.30 am	Work stopped owing to heavy shell fire and direct hit on Gun pit and four on the sides, Gun half buried.	
		2pm	Reported to Headquarters R.A. impossible to get Gun into action ordered to withdraw the Battery into Dug outs at Q.30.b 80.30	#
			Casualties One Gunner (Shell Shock)	
Q.30.b 80.30	5th		Headquarters shelled ordered to withdraw the Battery to Billets leaving Guard at Q.30.b 80.30. Battery arrived in ALBERT. at 3.30 pm	#

Army Form C. 2118.

WAR DIARY
or
INTELLIGENCE SUMMARY

(Erase heading not required.)

Instructions regarding War Diaries and Intelligence Summaries are contained in F.S. Regs., Part II. and the Staff Manual respectively. Title Pages will be prepared in manuscript.

Place	Date	Hour	Summary of Events and Information	Remarks and references to Appendices
ALBERT	6th		Battery at rest in Billets.	
ALBERT	7th		One Officer and 20 other ranks sent to THIEPVAL WOOD to salvage Guns at Q30 D 60.10 and Q30 D 70.35. O.C. reconnoitred THIEPVAL with a view to putting in a Gun but found it impossible	
ALBERT	8th		Party still salvaging guns in THIEPVAL WOOD. Battery preparing to move	
W18 6 30.70	9th		Battery moved into old gun positions at W18 6 30.70 and party sent to continue work in THIEPVAL WOOD and finished as 4-30 pm. O.C. ordered to reconnoitre for a new position in THIEPVAL WOOD, no position within range could be found.	
W18 6 30.70	10th to 13th		Battery at rest. Position shelled each night	
W18 6 30.70	14th		Battery ordered to help 82nd & 83rd Bde R.F.A. at new gun positions near MOUQUET FARM. men worked all night. Casualties One Corporal wounded	

Army Form C. 2118

WAR DIARY
or
INTELLIGENCE SUMMARY
(Erase heading not required.)

Instructions regarding War Diaries and Intelligence Summaries are contained in F.S. Regs., Part II. and the Staff Manual respectively. Title Pages will be prepared in manuscript.

Place	Date	Hour	Summary of Events and Information	Remarks and references to Appendices
W 18 b 30.70	15th		Guns all returned and received.	#
W 18 b 30.70	16th to 18th		Battery dipping new gun pits for 82nd RFA. One new gun arrived on the 18th	##
W 18 b 30.70	18th to 31st		Party supplied each day to 82nd Bde R.F.A. Battery running Gun Drill etc	##

Hayfield Capt RFA
Commanding V/118 Heavy Trench Mortar Battery R.H.

1875 Wt. W593/826 1,000,000 4/15 J.B.C. & A. A.D.S.S./Forms/C. 2118.

Copy

To Headquarters   V126
R.a. 18th Div.   2.10.16

According to your instructions T.B. 1144 the Battery under my command has relieved W/49 H.T.M. Bty today. The positions occupied by the Battery are as follows:-

1. 2 Gun Positions at Q 24 c 80.50
   1 " " Q 30 b 75.70

Of these positions 1 Gun has been completely knocked out and Gun out of action, the other has been buried three times and at present half buried. The whole of the position has been and is badly shelled most of the Dug Outs have been knocked in. W/49 suffering a good many casualties.

2. This Gun is out of action owing to it shooting over THIEPVAL the Gun is intact and I think the position could be altered to enable the Gun

contd

The other Gun was in its emplacement, which has been shelled, but the Gun intact.

I do not know what parts are missing, nor how much ammunition there is with these two Guns.

Could I be informed please whether I am to have these two Guns collected and withdrawn as they have not been handed over.

I shall await further instructions before doing anything, they will require a large Fatigue Party to extract them.

If it is thought necessary I could be present at Headquarters after the Court Martial tomorrow morning at 11 a.m.

L. Hayfield
Capt R.F.A.
comdg X/68 B

cont'd

to shoot over N.W. corner of SCHWABEN redoubt, although I am of the opinion that owing to the English ammunition it could be dangerous to our own Infantry.
At present I have two detachments in no 1 position under 2nd Lt Allen who is in direct communication with Battalion HQrs West Kents and I have arranged to keep an Orderly with H.Q 55 Inf. Brigade. I myself will be at no 1 position after 12 noon tomorrow.
The O.C. V/49 also took me round the two positions of V/49 at Q 30 D 60.10 and Q 30 D 70.25. There was however no one there; in this position 1 Gun was knocked out and parts of it lying about.

Vol 5.

CONFIDENTIAL

WAR-DIARY of

V/18 Heavy Trench Mortar Battery

from 1st November 1916 to 30th November 1916

(Volume VII)

Army Form C. 2118.

WAR DIARY
INTELLIGENCE SUMMARY
(Erase heading not required.)

Place	Date	Hour	Summary of Events and Information	Remarks and references to Appendices
In dug outs at W.18.C.30.y.d.	NOVEMBER 1916. 1st & -18th		Battery training and supplying fatigues for Artillery.	
do.	19th		Battery engaged in Artillery fatigues. One 9.45 Heavy Trench Mortar handed over and sent to Vth ARMY TRENCH MORTAR SCHOOL	
do.	20th to 25th		Half the battery salvaging guns at THIEPVAL WOOD (Two and one half guns salvaged and sent to I.O.M. IInd CORPS) Remainder of battery engaged in fatigues at Ammunition Dump.	
do.	26th & 27th		Fatigues at Ammunition Dump.	
do.	28th		Seventeen N.C.O.'s and men joined the battery as reinforcements. Fatigues at Ammunition Dump.	
do.	29th & 30th		Battery fatigues at Ammunition Dump.	

J Anglitt Lieut. RFA
Com'd'g V/19 H.T.M. Battery R.H.

Vol 6

Confidential

War Diary of

V/18 Heavy Trench Mortar Battery

from 1st December 1916 to 31st December 1916

(Volume VI.)

Army Form C. 2118.

WAR DIARY
INTELLIGENCE SUMMARY.
(Erase heading not required.)

Instructions regarding War Diaries and Intelligence Summaries are contained in F. S. Regs., Part II. and the Staff Manual respectively. Title pages will be prepared in manuscript.

Place	Date	Hour	Summary of Events and Information	Remarks and references to Appendices
	DECEMBER			
AVELUY	1st		Battery fatigues	#
W.18.C.30.40	2nd		Battery preparing to move	#
	3rd	8.30 a.m.	Battery moved by motor lorries to PETIT PORT, arriving there at 7.0 p.m.	#
PETIT PORT	4–11th		Battery training and fatigues at PORT LE GRAND	#
	11th	10.0 a.m.	Battery left billets at PETIT PORT, and proceeded to billets at GRAND LAVIERS.	#
GRAND LAVIERS	12–27th		Battery training, and erecting Nissen Huts for Artillery Brigades	#
	28th		Orders received to proceed into the line.	#
			Battery preparing to move	#
	29th	10 a.m.	Battery marched to ABBEVILLE and entrained for ACHEUX at 10.30 a.m.	#

WAR DIARY

INTELLIGENCE SUMMARY.

(Erase heading not required.)

Army Form C. 2118.

Place	Date	Hour	Summary of Events and Information	Remarks and references to Appendices
	DECEMBER			
	29th	8.30 p.m	On 8.30 p.m the battery detrained, and stayed the night in rest camp at ACHEUX	#
ACHEUX	30th	10.30am	Battery marched from ACHEUX to camp at V.12.C.4.5, remaining under canvas.	##
V.12.C.4.5	31st		The Battery was engaged in cutting timber at AVELUY WOOD	###

J Huythill Capt R.F.A.
O.C. 1/1 H.J.M Batt

Vol 7

CONFIDENTIAL

War Diary of

V/18 Heavy Trench Mortar Battery

from January 1st 1917 to January 31st 1917

(Volume VII)

Confidential

To.
Headquarters
R.A. 18th Divn.

V/18
HEAVY TRENCH
MORTAR BATTERY, R.A.
No. V465
... 5.2.17

Enclosed herewith War Diary for V/18 H.T.M. Batty for the month of January 1917. Please acknowledge.

5.2.17.

W Boak
for O.C. V/18 H.T.M. Batty

Army Form C. 2118.

WAR DIARY
INTELLIGENCE SUMMARY.
(Erase heading not required.)

Instructions regarding War Diaries and Intelligence Summaries are contained in F. S. Regs., Part II. and the Staff Manual respectively. Title pages will be prepared in manuscript.

Place	Date 1917	Hour	Summary of Events and Information	Remarks and references to Appendices
AVELUY WOOD.	January 1st	10.0 a.m.	The Battery marched from camp at V.12.c.4.5. to AVELUY WOOD remaining under canvas	6MB
"	1st–31st		Twenty-one other ranks were engaged on fatigues at PIONEER DUMP, under 2/Lt. F. ALLEN. The remainder were engaged in felling trees in AVELUY FOREST, and splitting logs for gun positions, cutting poles for Brigade + D.A.C. Wagon lines, and also cutting Telephone Poles.	6MB
"	18th		Two N.C.O's and eight men proceeded to Camp in AUTHUILLE WOOD, for purpose of preparing gun positions for the 84th Bde. R.F.A.	6MB
"	22nd		One N.C.O. and ten men were detached for fatigues at IInd CORPS AMMUNITION DUMP, DONNET'S POST.	6MB
"	23rd		Capt. L. HAYBITTEL and one N.C.O. proceeded to Vth ARMY TRENCH MORTAR SCHOOL	4MB
"	30th		The fatigue Party of 2 N.C.O's and 8 men with 84th BDE. R.F.A. returned to camp in AVELUY WOOD	4MB

[signed] for O.C. V/18 H.T.M. Batt.

CONFIDENTIAL

War Diary of

V/18 Heavy Trench Mortar Battery

from 1st February 1917 to 28th February 1917

(Volume VIII)

Army Form. C. 2118.

WAR DIARY
INTELLIGENCE SUMMARY

(Erase heading not required.)

Instructions regarding War Diaries and Intelligence Summaries are contained in F. S. Regs., Part II. and the Staff Manual respectively. Title Pages will be prepared in manuscript.

Place	Date February 1917	Hour	Summary of Events and Information	Remarks and references to Appendices
AVELUY WOOD	1st–28th		One N.C.O. and ten men were engaged on Ammunition Fatigues at DONNETS POST	
	1st–24th		Fifteen other ranks were engaged in fatigues at PIONEER DUMP under 2/Lt. T.F. ALLEN. The remainder were employed in fatigues in AVELUY WOOD.	
	7th		CAPT. L. HAYBITTEL returned from $\overline{V^{th}}$ ARMY TRENCH MORTAR SCHOOL	
	25th–28th		Twenty four other ranks were engaged in preparing gun positions for 18th DIV. ARTILLERY, and Ammunition fatigues.	

Capt. R.F.A.
O.C. V/18 H.T.M. Batt'y

Vol. 10

Copy.

Confidential

War Diary of

V/18 Heavy Trench Mortar Battery

from 1st February 1917 to 28th February 1917.

(Volume VIII)

Army Form C. 2118.

WAR DIARY
INTELLIGENCE SUMMARY
(Erase heading not required.)

copy

Instructions regarding War Diaries and Intelligence Summaries are contained in F. S. Regs., Part II. and the Staff Manual respectively. Title Pages will be prepared in manuscript.

Place	Date February 1917	Hour	Summary of Events and Information	Remarks and references to Appendices
AVELUY WOOD	1-28th		One N.C.O. and ten men were engaged on Ammunition fatigues at DONNET'S POST	
	1-24th		Fifteen other ranks were engaged in fatigues at PIONEER DUMP under 2/Lt F. ALLEN. The remainder were employed in fatigues in AVELUY WOOD.	
	7th		CAPT. L. HAYBITTEL returned from Vth ARMY TRENCH MORTAR SCHOOL	
	25-28th		Twenty four other ranks were engaged in preparing gun positions for 18th DIV. ARTILLERY, and Ammunition fatigues	

A. N[...]
Capt R.F.A.
O.C. V/18 H.T.M.B att

Vol

Confidential

War Diary

of

V/18 Heavy Trench Mortar Battery R.A.

From March 1st 1917 To March 31st 1917

(Volume IX)

Army Form C. 2118.

WAR DIARY
or
INTELLIGENCE SUMMARY

(Erase heading not required.)

Place	Date	Hour	Summary of Events and Information	Remarks and references to Appendices
AVELUY WOOD	1st March to 5th March		One N.C.O and 10 other ranks still detached and on fatigues at II Corps Ammunition Dump. Remainder on Ammunition Fatigues for 18th Division Artillery.	AH
AVELUY WOOD	6th		Ordered to move Battery to R32d0.8. and occupy old enemy dugouts	AH
	11	3.P.M.	Battery moved and settled in dugouts	
R32d0.8 DUGOUTS	7th		All men employed on Ammunition Fatigues	AH
		12 mid-night	Received orders from H.Q. R.A to be prepared to move the whole Battery at 8.A.M next morning to join 3rd ARMY.	
R32d0.9 DUGOUT	8th	8.A.M.	Battery moved by motor lorries with orders to report to 17th Corps Siege Park at SAVY. One N.C.O & 10 other ranks on II Corps ammunition dump reopened the Battery before moving. Route passed for motor lorries — AVELUY. — HEDAUVILLE. — CONTAY. — TALMAS. — DOULLENS. — LUCHEUX. — AVESNES- le- COMTE. — SAVY.	AH
		8.30.P.M	Battery arrived at 17th Corps Siege Park and ordered by 17th Corps Q. to proceed to AUBIGNY.	
		9.30	Battery arrived at AUBIGNY and billeted in "Rest Camp".	AH

Army Form C. 2118.

WAR DIARY
INTELLIGENCE SUMMARY

(Erase heading not required.)

Instructions regarding War Diaries and Intelligence Summaries are contained in F.S. Regs., Part II. and the Staff Manual respectively. Title Pages will be prepared in manuscript.

Place	Date	Hour	Summary of Events and Information	Remarks and references to Appendices
AUBIGNY.	9th		Battery at "Rest Camp" awaiting orders.	H
AUBIGNY.	10th	10.AM	Four motor lorries sent to SAVY to collect 4 – 9.45" Trench Mortars at 17th Corps Seige Park.	H
		4.30 P.M	Battery moved in motor lorries with guns to ARRAS and joined 9th Division Trench Mortars	
		10. P.M	Battery billeted in ARRAS.	
ARRAS.	11th to 12th		Battery overhauling guns and stores	H
ARRAS	13th		V/9 H.T.M. Battery handed over one gun complete in emplacement at G.17.d.01.50 also two incomplete emplacements at G.17.b.30.90.	H
ARRAS	14th		All men employed helping Engineers on emplacements at G.17.b.30.90	H
ARRAS	15th	1.30 P.M	Fired 10 rounds from gun at G.17.d.01.50 – Two direct hits on enemy trenches at G.18.b.10.45. Remainder of battery employed on other positions	H
ARRAS	16th	1.30 P.M	Fired 8 rounds from gun at G.17.d.01.50. Short stopped owing to enemy aircraft	H
		3. P.M	Position heavily shelled by enemy with 5.9 guns, one direct hit on ammunition pit, rest gun pit slightly	

Army Form C. 2118.

WAR DIARY
or
INTELLIGENCE SUMMARY
(Erase heading not required.)

Place	Date	Hour	Summary of Events and Information	Remarks and references to Appendices
ARRAS	17th		One gun taken up & put in left hand emplacement at G.17.b.30.90.	A
		5.30 P.M.	Gun ready for firing. Ammunition put at G.17.d.01.50. upwind.	
ARRAS	18th	1.30 P.M.	Fired 4 rounds from gun at G.17.b.30.90. Telephone wire between this gun & O.P. (House at G.23.c.35.15) cut in 11 places by enemy shells (4.2). and stopped short.	A
ARRAS	19th		Battery on carrying up ammunition to emplacements at G.17.b.30.90 & G.17.d.01.50. 50 rounds of ammunition carried up to this position.	A
ARRAS	20th		One gun taken up & put in right hand emplacement at G.17.b.30.90. also had batten.	A
		11 P.M.	Gun ready for firing.	
ARRAS	21st		Work on emplacements & ammunition pit progressing.	A
ARRAS	22nd	1.30 P.M.	Fire 10 rounds – 5 from each gun at G.17.b.30.90. Observation bad owing to snow storm. Work continued on emplacements. 9 Gunners proceeded from 98 S.A.C.	A
ARRAS	23rd	1.30 P.M.	Fired 10 rounds from right hand gun at G.17.b.30.90. Three direct hits observed on enemy trench, one German seen to climb out of trench but ran across opened. Work on emplacements continued.	A

Army Form C. 2118.

WAR DIARY
or
INTELLIGENCE SUMMARY
(Erase heading not required.)

Instructions regarding War Diaries and Intelligence Summaries are contained in F. S. Regs., Part II. and the Staff Manual respectively. Title Pages will be prepared in manuscript.

Place	Date	Hour	Summary of Events and Information	Remarks and references to Appendices
ARRAS	24th	1.15. night	Fired 5 round from left hand gun at G17b 30.90 at enemy trenches. Handed over gun and emplacements at G.17d 01.50 to V/4 H.T.M. Battery R.A.	A
ARRAS	25th		Working on ammunition pits at G.17 b 30.90.	A
ARRAS	26th	12.P.M	Fired 5 rounds left hand gun at G17 b 30.90. at enemy trenches. Works continued on ammunition pits.	A
ARRAS	27th	3.PM	Fired 10 rounds left hand gun at G.17 b 30.90 at enemy trench, dug out hit. Work continued on ammunition pits.	A
ARRAS	28th to 30th		Ammunition pits completed. 200 rounds of ammunition carried up to emplacements.	A
ARRAS	31st	12.30 P.M	Fired 10 rounds from left hand gun at G.17 b 30.90 at enemy O.P. (G 12 d 05.75). One round hit enemy small ammunition dump on trench, several small explosions heard.	A

D. Hayflett Capt R.F.A
O.C V/18 H.T.M Battery R.A

2449 Wt. W14957/M90 750,000 1/16 J.B.C. & A. Forms/C.2118/22.

Confidential

War Diary of

V/18 Heavy Trench Mortar Battery.

from 1st APRIL 1917 to 30th APRIL 1917.

(Volume X)

WAR DIARY
INTELLIGENCE SUMMARY

(Erase heading not required.)

Army Form C. 2118.

Place	Date	Hour	Summary of Events and Information	Remarks and references to Appendices
ARRAS	APRIL 1st	12 noon	Guns at G.17.b.30.90. Given code names:- Right hand gun - MAC: Left hand gun - LIZZ. Fired 21 rounds at Enemy O.P.- G.12.d.05.15. Target damaged.	A
	2nd	12 noon	Fired 11 rounds from MAC at same O.P. Ammunition taken up to guns to complete 200 per gun.	A
	3rd	10.30 am	Urgent orders received from 18th D.T.M.O - "V" day tomorrow, 4th inst. LT. W.T. BOSTON sent up in charge of MAC gun, with Y N.C.O's and men. 2/LT. F. ALLEN sent up in charge of LIZZ gun, with Y N.C.O's and men. Reserve detachment sent to cellar in ST. NICHOLAS. The O.C. took up his headquarters at the O.P.- house at G.23.C.35.15, with 4 telephonists and one other rank. Remainder of battery in billets in ARRAS. Programme of fire (appendix V.1) given to both Section Commanders with instructions should telephone communications be cut off, programme to be adhered to, unless otherwise ordered.	A
	4th V day	7.45 pm	Both guns fired as per programme Orders issued to Section Commanders (appendix V.2) by O.C.	A

Army Form C. 2118.

WAR DIARY
— or —
INTELLIGENCE SUMMARY
(Erase heading not required.)

Instructions regarding War Diaries and Intelligence Summaries are contained in F. S. Regs., Part II. and the Staff Manual respectively. Title Pages will be prepared in manuscript.

Place	Date APRIL	Hour	Summary of Events and Information	Remarks and references to Appendices
ARRAS	4th Viny	8.0 p.m.	Officer in charge MAC sent orders re firing (appendix V.3) by O.C. Alteration to programme of fire sent to Section Commanders (appendix V.4) from O.C.	#
	5th W day	8.30 a.m. 8.40 p.m.	Orders sent to Section Commanders re firing (appendix V.5) by O.C. Alteration to programme of fire sent to Section Commanders (appendix V.6) from O.C.	#
	6th X day	1.0 p.m. 8.0 p.m.	Received orders bombardment will last an extra day and be called "Q" day. Section Commanders ordered over telephone to decrease fire to 4 rounds per hour instead of 6 rounds per hour. Alteration to programme of fire sent to Section Commanders (appendix V.7) "V" with 4:2. Enemy shelled O.P. Orders issued to Officer in charge MAC, re shortening of fuzes (appendix V.7a) by O.C.	#
	7th Q day	1.00 a.m. 5.30 p.m.	O.C. ordered MAC to switch to fresh target, reported to be a strong point, and controlled fire on to target until successfully engaged. O.C. ordered MAC to switch to another target (target O - G.12.d.05.35) "minenwerfer" emplacements. Range — Elevation 62½°. Fuze 19¼. Line 3.30° M.R.	#

Army Form C. 2118.

WAR DIARY
INTELLIGENCE SUMMARY
(Erase heading not required.)

Instructions regarding War Diaries and Intelligence Summaries are contained in F. S. Regs., Part II. and the Staff Manual respectively. Title Pages will be prepared in manuscript.

Place	Date	Hour	Summary of Events and Information	Remarks and references to Appendices
ARRAS	APRIL 7th (Q day)	5.30pm 8.20pm	One direct hit observed. Alteration to programme of fire sent to section commanders (appendix V.8.) Enemy shelled O.P. with 4.2".	///
	8th "Y day"	7.0pm 8.45pm	Orders received from 18th D.T.M.O. Zero hour fixed 5.30 a.m. tomorrow 9th inst. Orders sent to Section Commanders re withdrawal. (appendix V.9.) Enemy shelled O.P. Direct hit 77mm field gun. Enemy shelled positions with 5.9", & 4.2". One shell damaging entrance to passage way, wounding one gunner.	///
	9th Z day	6.30am	Lt. BOSTON and detachment returned to billets in ARRAS. Direct hit on billet by 4.2" shell wounding three gunners.	///
	10th		Two guns fallen out of positions, brought back, and handed over to 9th DIV.	///
	11th–27th		Battery remaining in billets in ARRAS at rest. Kit and equipment inspections.	///

Army Form C. 2118.

WAR DIARY
or
INTELLIGENCE SUMMARY

(Erase heading not required.)

Instructions regarding War Diaries and Intelligence Summaries are contained in F. S. Regs., Part II. and the Staff Manual respectively. Title Pages will be prepared in manuscript.

Place	Date APRIL	Hour	Summary of Events and Information	Remarks and references to Appendices
ARRAS	28th		Orders to report 18th DIVN. received from XVII. Corps. Battery left ARRAS, in motor-lorries and arrived at OBLINGHAM at 12.30 p.m. finding that the Division had left the 3rd ARMY. Proceeded thence to PERNES and received instructions from "Q" Branch 18th DIVN. Battery billeted in PERNES for the night and proceeded by motor lorries next morning to join the 7th Corps.	A
PERNES	29th	9.30 a.m.	The battery moved by motor-lorries from PERNES, proceeded to BEAURAINS and bivouaced. Came under orders of 18th DIV. ART.Y.	A
BEAURAINS	30th		Battery at rest.	A

A.Hoylett.
Capt. R.F.A.
O.C. V/18 H.T.M. Batty

APPENDIX V.I.

Programme of Fire by Capt. L. Haybittel.
Comdg. V/18 Heavy Trench Mortar Battery

Time	Rate of fire	Targets	Range etc		
V day 9.A.M to 12.30 P.M	4 rounds	(MAC) (No 3 Gun) U, Y + X	U.F.18.9 Y.F.19.9 X.F.20.1	E 59¼ E 65½ E 67	Line Zero 0° M.R 7° M.R
4 P.M to 6. P.M.	per hour	V + W	V.F 20 W.F. 20.3	E 66¾ E 68½	1° M.R 3° M.R
V day 12.30 P.M to 4.P.M	4 rounds	No 2 Gun (LIZ) A, B + E	A.F. 17 B.F. 18.5	E 50¼ E 57	Line Zero 3° M.R
6. P.M. to 8. P.M.	per hour	A + F.	E.F. 19.7 F.F. 18.5	E 64 E 57	6° M.R 9°.30 M.R
MAC to fire 18 rounds at night if ordered			F. 16	E 50¼	Zero
W day 5.A.M to 9.A.M	4 rounds	(LIZ) F + E			
1.P.M to 4.30.P.M	per hour	A,C + F.	C.F.18.9	E 59¼	Line 2°.30 M.R
W day 9.A.M to 1.P.M	4 rounds	(MAC) U² + Z.	U².F.17 Z.F.20.5	E 50¼ E 69¾	Line Zero. 8° M.R
4.30. P.M. to 8.P.M.	per hour	Y.V + T	T.F.20.7	E 69¾	13° M.R
LIZ to fire 18 rounds at night if ordered.			F.16.	E 50¼	10°. M.R
X day 5.A.M to 9.A.M	6 rounds	(MAC) U + W			
1.P.M to 4.30.P.M	per hour	U² V + W			
X day 9.A.M to 1.P.M	6 rounds	(LIZ) B + F.			
4.30 P.M to 8.P.M	per hour	A.C. + d	d.F.18.9	E 59¼	Line 1°. M.R.
MAC to fire 18 rounds at night if ordered			F. 16	E 50¼.	Zero.
Y day 5.A.M. to 9.A.M.	6 rounds	(LIZ) A² + F	A².F.17.5	E 52¼	Line 1° M.R.
1.P.M to 4.30 P.M	per hour	A,d + F			
Y day 9.A.M to 1.P.M.	6 rounds	(MAC) Y + T			
4.30 P.M to 8.0 P.M.	per hour	U + S	S.F.19.2	E 61¼	Line 2° M.L
LIZ to fire 18 rounds at night if ordered			F.16.	E 50¼	Line Zero
Z day. MAC and LIZ to have 2 rounds on hand for ZERO hour if required, and will each fire 1 round at zero hour if ordered.			LIZ F.17 MAC F.17	E 50¼ E 50¼	Line 10° M.R. Line Zero.

April 3rd 17.

L Haybittel Capt
R.F.A.
Comdg V/18 H.T.M. Battery
R.A

APPENDIX V.2.

Alteration to Programme of Fire

Rate of fire for tomorrow 5th inst. (W'day) altered from 4 rounds per hour to 6 rounds.

Target E for LIZZ is cancelled, and replaced by target G.

G — Fuze 19. Elevation 69¼ Line 6° M.R

Add 6 sec. to all Fuzes give expect for night firing

L. Huybuttel
Capt R.F.A
O.C. 'Fatigue'

4-4-17.
7.45pm

APPENDIX V.3

Officer i/c MAC.

MAC will fire 18 rounds tonight after 12 midnight at the rate of 6 rounds per hour

April 4th 1917
8.0 p.m.

S. Anyhitt
Capt R.F.A.
O.C. Fatigue

APPENDIX. V.4.

OFFICER i/c LIZZ
OFFICER i/c MAC.

LIZZ will not fire between the hours of 7.50 A.M. and 9. A.M. unless otherwise ordered.
MAC will start firing at 9.0 A.M. unless otherwise ordered.
This alteration is due to "CHINESE ATTACK."

April 4"/17
8.0 p.m.

[signature] Capt R.F.A.
O.C. Fatigue

APPENDIX V.5.

OFFICER i/c MAC
OFFICER i/c LIZZ

MAC will not fire between 10.A.M and 10.30 A.M today (W day).

LIZZ will not fire between 3.P.M & 3.30 P.M today (W day)

These pauses are for the purpose of Photographing

5-4-17
8.30 A.M.

D. Hayhurst
Capt RFA
OC. Fatigue.

APPENDIX. 6.

Alterations to Programme of fire

LIZZ will fire tonight but not between the hours of 11 P.M. to 1.A.M. and will only fire 9 rounds.

X day. April 6th.

LIZZ will not fire between 10.30.A.M. and 11.A.M.
MAC will not fire between 3.p.m. and 3.30 p.m.
These pauses are for the purpose of Photographing.
There is no "CHINESE" Attack, but MAC will not fire between 1.30 p.m and 1.40 p.m.
At 1.40 p.m MAC will fire one round as at ZERO hour and then continue programme

L Haybittle
Capt R.F.A.
O.C. Fatigue

April 5th/17.
8.40. P.M.

APPENDIX. V. 7.

Alterations to Programme of fire
April 6th/17

MAC will fire 9 rounds tonight, but not between the hours 10.p.m and 12.0 p.m.

Q day April 7th

Programme for Q day will be the same as Y day except rate of fire :- rate of fire 4 rounds per hour.
LIZZ will open fire at 6.A.M. instead of 5.A.M and will not fire more than at the rate of 4 per hour.
MAC will stop firing at 7.P.M. instead of 8. p m and save 4 rounds.
MAC will not fire between the hours of 11.15 A.M. & 11.30.A.M.

April 6/17
8. p.m

L. Haylittle
Capt R.F.A
O.C. FATIGUE

OFFICER i/c MAC.   (Appendix V.7a)

Shorten all fuzes to 4".5.
All Fuzes now as per programme.

L Hayhutt
Capt RHA
O.C. 'Fatigue'

6-4-17.

APPENDIX. V. 8

Alteration to Programme of Fire

LIZZ. will fire 18 rounds tonight but not between the hours 9.P.M. to 11 P.M.

Y day April 8th/17.

MAC.
6.A.M. – 10.A.M.   Targets O.U² + S
2.P.M. – 5.P.M.   "   X.U + Y

LIZZ
10.A.M to 2.0 P.M   A.F.C
5.0 P.M. to 8. P.M.   B.G.C.

} Rate of fire 6 rounds per hour

LIZZ will not fire between the hours of 11.15 A.M to 11.30 A.M. At 11.30 will fire one round as on Z day at zero hour.

April 7th/17
8.20. P.M.

L Haythuttel
Capt R.F.A
O.C. Fangue

~~OFFICER i/c MAC~~ tk.   Appendix V.9.
OFFICER i/c. LIZZ.

You and your detachment must return to billets in ARRAS tonight.

           L Haylittel   Capt R.F.A
April 8th 17.   O.C. Fatigue.
8.45 p.m.

(APPENDIX V.10)

OFFICER i/c MAC

After the completion of your duties, you and your detachment will return to billets in ARRAS tomorrow morning.

April 8th 1917
8.45 pm

L. Huylittle
Capt R.F.A.
O.C. Fatigue

Confidential

War Diary of

V/18 Heavy Trench Mortar Battery

from 1st May 1917 to 31st May 1917

(Volume XI)

Army Form C. 2118.

WAR DIARY
INTELLIGENCE SUMMARY.
(Erase heading not required.)

Instructions regarding War Diaries and Intelligence Summaries are contained in F. S. Regs, Part II. and the Staff Manual respectively. Title pages will be prepared in manuscript.

Place	Date MAY 1917	Hour	Summary of Events and Information	Remarks and references to Appendices
BEAURAINS	1st-25th		Battery resting, training and equipped.	
- do -	26th		One N.C.O and 5 men attached to A/82nd Bde R.F.A for fatigues	
			" " " D/82 " " "	
			" " " A/83 " " "	
- do -			One N.C.O and Y " " B/83 " " "	
			" " " C/83 " " "	
- do -	27th		One gunner killed, two wounded, and one gunner wounded and remaining at duty, at D/82nd Bde R.F.A	
- do -	29th		Two N.C.O.s and two men attached to D/82nd Bde R.F.A	
- do -	31st		N.C.O.s and men still attached to above field Batteries	

[signature] Major R.F.A
O.C. V/18 M.T.M.Bg.

T134. Wt. W708—776. 500000. 4/15. Sir J.C. & S.

Confidential

War Diary of

V/18 Heavy Trench Mortar Battery

from 1st June 1917 to 30th June 1917

(Volume XII)

Army Form C. 2118.

June 1917.

WAR DIARY
INTELLIGENCE SUMMARY.
(Erase heading not required.)

Instructions regarding War Diaries and Intelligence Summaries are contained in F.S. Regs., Part II. and the Staff Manual respectively. Title pages will be prepared in manuscript.

Place	Date	Hour	Summary of Events and Information	Remarks and references to Appendices
BEAURAINS	1st June		Battery preparing to move	##
	2nd		Battery moved to HENIN-SUR-COJEUL and bivouaced. One 9.45" Heavy Trench Mortar transported and taken over from III'd Army Trench Mortar School.	##
HENIN-SUR-COJEUL	3rd		Twenty four N.C.O's and men returned from Batteries of 82nd and 83rd Bdes R.F.A, leaving 18 N.C.O's and men still attached for fatigues	##
	4th-17th		Twenty N.C.O's and men assisted R.E's in preparing trench mortar Emplacement at O.31.6.58.	##
"	18th		Trench Mortar and Emplacement handed over to 50th DIVN.	##
"	19-26th		Battery training	##

WAR DIARY

INTELLIGENCE SUMMARY
(Erase heading not required.)

Army Form C. 2118.

JUNE 1917.

Place	Date JUNE	Hour	Summary of Events and Information	Remarks and references to Appendices
HENIN-SUR-COJEUL	22		Remainder of N.C.O's and men returned from batteries of 82nd and 83rd Bdes. R.F.A.	#
	27th	9.45 a.m	Battery marched to rest camp at HENDECOURT-LES-RANSART.	#
HENDECOURT-LES-RANSART	28th-30th		Battery at rest.	#

A. Lyttel, Capt R.F.A
O.C. C/118 A.I.m Bty

Confidential

War Diary of

V/18 Heavy Trench Mortar Battery

From 1st July 1917 to 31st July 1917

(Volume XIII)

Army Form C. 2118.

WAR DIARY
INTELLIGENCE SUMMARY.
(Erase heading not required.)

Instructions regarding War Diaries and Intelligence Summaries are contained in F. S. Regs., Part II. and the Staff Manual respectively. Title pages will be prepared in manuscript.

Place	Date JULY	Hour	Summary of Events and Information	Remarks and references to Appendices
HENDECOURT	3rd 1+2		Battery at rest	A
"	3rd	9.0am	Battery proceeded by motor lorries to billets in DOULLENS	A
DOULLENS	4th	1.30pm	Battery Entrained, and arrived at GODEWAERSVELDE at 10.30 pm, and then marched to farm 2 kilometres South of STEENWOORDE and bivouaced.	A
STEENWOORDE	5th-11th		Battery at rest and training.	A
do.	12th	8.0am	Battery proceeded by motor lorries to camp at H.26.d.5.5. near DICKEBUSCH.	A
Camp at H.26.d.55	13th		One Officer and seventeen Other ranks proceeded to the line to help V.30 H.T.M.B.y construct trench mortar position.	A
do.	16th		Battery ordered to complete trench mortar position at RUSKIN HOUSE. I.24.c.05.20.	A

WAR DIARY

INTELLIGENCE SUMMARY.
(Erase heading not required.)

Army Form C. 2118.

Place	Date JULY	Hour	Summary of Events and Information	Remarks and references to Appendices
	17		The remainder of battery moved up to dug outs in embankment near ZILLEBEKE LAKE, I.21.b.9.9.0.5. Work started on position.	A
	18		Three direct hits on position and one gunner wounded. One officer and 16 other ranks returned to camp at H.26.d.5.5 from V/30 H.T.M.By.	A
	19 to 21		Work continued on position, which was heavily shelled. Two gunners wounded. Dug-outs shelled at night with gas shells. One gunner returned to camp slightly gassed.	A
	22-23		Work in progress on position. Two direct hits on ammunition recess which was knocked in.	A
	23	3.0 a.m.	Orders received for remainder of battery to return to camp at H.26.d.5.5.	A

Army Form C. 2118.

WAR DIARY

INTELLIGENCE SUMMARY.

(Erase heading not required.)

Instructions regarding War Diaries and Intelligence
Summaries are contained in F. S. Regs., Part II.
and the Staff Manual respectively. Title pages
will be prepared in manuscript.

Place	Date	Hour	Summary of Events and Information	Remarks and references to Appendices
	JULY			
H.26.d.5.5	24-30		Fatigue parties supplied each night for Ammunition Dump.	
-do-	31		Battery detailed to act as stretcher bearer parties.	

A Whytehead Capt R.F.A.
O.C. V/118 T.M.By

Confidential

War Diary of

V/18 Heavy Trench Mortar Battery.

From 1st August 1917 to 31st August 1917

Army Form C. 2118.

WAR DIARY
INTELLIGENCE SUMMARY.
(Erase heading not required.)

Instructions regarding War Diaries and Intelligence Summaries are contained in F. S. Regs., Part II. and the Staff Manual respectively. Title pages will be prepared in manuscript.

Place	Date AUGUST	Hour	Summary of Events and Information	Remarks and references to Appendices
Campal H.26.d.55	28		Thirty four other ranks attached to 18th Divl Field Batteries for fatigues.	
do	29th		CAPT. L. HAYBITTEL posted to 83rd Bde R.F.A. LIEUT D.G. MEDUS posted to V/18 H.T.M.BATTY. from X/18 T.M.BATTY. and assumed command.	
do	30th	7.30 a.m.	Remainder of Battery proceeded by motor lorries to OUDERZEELE and encamped.	
OUDERZEELE	31st		Fatigue parties of N.C.O.s and men returned from field Batteries	

D.G. Medus Lt. R.F.A.
Comdg V/18 H.T.M.Batty.

Army Form C. 2118.

WAR DIARY
—or—
INTELLIGENCE SUMMARY

(Erase heading not required.)

V/18A.T.M.BY

Vol 15

September 1917

Place	Date	Hour	Summary of Events and Information	Remarks and references to Appendices
OUDEZEELE	1st–19th		Battery at rest and training	
"	20th		Battery moved by motor lorries to SERQUES, rest area, and encamped	
SERQUES	20th–23rd		Battery training	
"	24th		Battery moved by motor lorries to billets at ZEGGERS-CAPPEL	
ZEGGERS-CAPPEL	25th	3.0 p.m.	Battery moved by motor lorries to forward area at POPERINGHE.	
POPERINGHE	26th & 27th		Battery training.	
"	28th		Battery marched to VLAMERTINGHE and took over billets vacated by 48th Divl TRENCH MORTARS CAPT D.G. MEDUS and two N.C.O.'s proceeded to V Army Trench Mortar School for Heavy Trench Mortar Course.	
VLAMERTINGHE	29th		Battery training	
- do -	30th		Fatigue party of 20 N.C.O's & men supplied to 84th Bde A.F.A for fatigues. Fatigue party of 5 N.C.O's & men supplied to 290th Bde. R.F.A. 48th DIVN for fatigues	

[signature]
for O.C. V/18A.T.M.By

[signature] Capt R.F.A.
V/18A T.M. By

Army Form C. 2118.

OCTOBER 1917.

WAR DIARY of V/18 A.I.M. Batty

INTELLIGENCE SUMMARY.

(Erase heading not required.)

Instructions regarding War Diaries and Intelligence Summaries are contained in F. S. Regs., Part II. and the Staff Manual respectively. Title pages will be prepared in manuscript.

Place	Date	Hour	Summary of Events and Information	Remarks and references to Appendices
VLAMERTINGHE	1-6			
	7th		Fatigue party of 20 N.C.O.s + men remaining with 84th Bde. R.F.A.	
			Fatigue party of 5 N.C.O.s + men remaining with 290th Bde. R.F.A.	
	7th		Fatigue party returned from 290th Bde. R.F.A.	
	8th		Fatigue party returned from 84th Bde. A.F.A.	
	11		Sixteen N.C.O.s + men attached to ZOUAVE VILLA DUMP.	
			One N.C.O. attached R.E. DUMP ZOUAVE VILLA.	
	12th		Two 9.45" Heavy Trench Mortars MkIII remaining in the line, taken over from 51st DIV.	
	13th		Battery marched to TROIS TOURS, and took over turrets vacated by 51st DIV. T.M.B.s.	
TROIS-TOURS	16th		CAPT D.G. MEDUS and two N.C.O.s returned from Vth Army I.M School	
	18th		One N.C.O and 4 men attached to B/83rd Bde R.F.A. for fatigues.	
	19th		CAPT D.G. MEDUS Engaged in salving Guns.	
	21		One N.C.O and 4 men returned from B/83rd Bde R.F.A.	
			Five N.C.O.s and men returned to B/83rd Bde R.F.A for duty	
			Five N.C.O.s and men attached to D/83rd Bde R.F.A for duty	

Army Form C. 2118.

WAR DIARY
INTELLIGENCE SUMMARY.

(Erase heading not required.)

OCTOBER 1917.

Place	Date	Hour	Summary of Events and Information	Remarks and references to Appendices
TROIS TOURS	24th		Fifteen other ranks returned from ZOUAVE VILLA DUMP.	
			Ten N.C.O.'s and men attached to D/83 Bde R.F.A	
	26th		Five N.C.O.'s and men attached to A/83 Bde R.F.A	
	28th		One Officer attached for duty with D/83 Bde R.F.A	
	31st		One Officer attached for duty with D/83 Bde R.F.A	
			Fatigue parties still attached to Brigades	

L.P. Wenlsbyn R.F.A.
Comdg V/18 H.T.M. Batt.

Army Form C. 2118.

WAR DIARY
or
INTELLIGENCE SUMMARY.
(Erase heading not required.)

Instructions regarding War Diaries and Intelligence Summaries are contained in F.S. Regs., Part II. and the Staff Manual respectively. Title pages will be prepared in manuscript.

V

178/4TM By
18D TM By
Sy 17

Place	Date	Hour	Summary of Events and Information	Remarks and references to Appendices
TROIS TOURS	NOVEMBER 1-20		Five other ranks attached D/82nd Bde R.F.A for fatigues. Two O.R's attached to D/83rd Bde R.F.A for fatigues. Three O.R's attached to A/82nd Bde R.F.A for fatigues. One N.C.O attached Ammunition Refilling Point. Twenty O.R's engaged in salvaging Field Guns.	
do	12th		Lieut W.T.BOSTON. R.F.A. transferred to D/82nd Bde R.F.A	
do	21st		Two N.C.O.'s proceeded to Vth Army Trench Mortar School for course of instruction	
do	28th		Fourteen reinforcements posted from 18th D.A.C	
do	29		Six reinforcements posted from 18th D.A.C to complete establishment	

8 Wolastapi R3a
O.C. V/18 A T.M By

T2134. Wt. W708—776. 500000. 4/15. Sir J.C. & S.

Army Form C. 2118.

WAR DIARY
INTELLIGENCE SUMMARY.
(Erase heading not required.)

V/18 H.T.M. Battery

DECEMBER 1917

Army Form C. 2118.

WAR DIARY
of V/18 H.T.M. By.
INTELLIGENCE SUMMARY.
(Erase heading not required.)

Place	Date	Hour	Summary of Events and Information	Remarks and references to Appendices
TROIS TOURS	1-10th		Battery Engaged in Salvaging guns and supplying fatigue parties to Field Batteries.	
	11th		Fatigue Parties rejoined Battery.	
	12th		Two 9.45" Heavy Trench Mortars (Mk II & III) handed over to 58th D.T.M.O.	
CROMBEKE	13th		Battery proceeded by motor lorries to CROMBEKE Rest Area.	
	14th-31st		Battery at rest and training	

Jallur Lieut R.F.A.
for O.C. V/18 H.T.M. By.

Army Form C. 2118.

WAR DIARY
or
INTELLIGENCE SUMMARY.
(Erase heading not required.)

Instructions regarding War Diaries and Intelligence Summaries are contained in F. S. Regs., Part II. and the Staff Manual respectively. Title pages will be prepared in manuscript.

Place	Date	Hour	Summary of Events and Information	Remarks and references to Appendices

T/134. Wt. W708—776. 500000. 4/15. Sir J. C. & S.

Army Form C. 2118

WAR DIARY
or
INTELLIGENCE SUMMARY

(Erase heading not required.)

War Diary of
V/18 Heavy Trench Mortar Batty
for January 1918.

Army Form C. 2118.

WAR DIARY
INTELLIGENCE SUMMARY

January 1918

(Erase heading not required.)

Instructions regarding War Diaries and Intelligence Summaries are contained in F. S. Regs., Part II. and the Staff Manual respectively. Title pages will be prepared in manuscript.

Place	Date	Hour	Summary of Events and Information	Remarks and references to Appendices
CROMBEKE	1st	7.30a	Battery moved by motor lorries from CROMBEKE to LARREY FARM, ELVERDINGHE. (Map. Ref. Sheet 28 N.W. B.9.C.1.4.)	
B.9.C.1.4.	3-4th		1 N.C.O. + 5 men attached to LUNAVILLE DUMP.	
"	5-24th		1 N.C.O. + 6 men attached to 82nd Bde H.Q., LAPIN FARM.	
"	5-14th 5-31st		3 N.C.O's and 17 men at STRAY FARM (Sheet 28 N.W. C.3.c.2.9.), Salvaging ammunition on divisional front.	
"	6-21st		One officer and twelve gunners attending 6" Newton and 9.45" Trench Mortar Course, LEULINGHEM.	
"	21st-29th		Ten other ranks attached 18th D.I.V.R.A. H.Q	

W. Good Capt R.G.A.
O.C. V/18th T. M. By.

T.2134. Wt. W708-776. 500000. 4/15. Sir J. C. & S.

XVIII

Vol 1

Confidential

War Diary

of

W/18 Heavy Trench Mortar Battery

from 21st May 1916 to 31st May 1916

(Volume I)

To The D.A.G.
3rd Echelon

Enclosed herewith War Diary of W/18. Heavy Trench Mortar Battery, covering period 21st-31st May/16.

Lt. R.F.A.
Comdg W/18. H.T.M. Batty

2/6/16

W24.

Army Form C. 2118.

WAR DIARY
or
INTELLIGENCE SUMMARY.
(Erase heading not required.)

Instructions regarding War Diaries and Intelligence Summaries are contained in F. S. Regs., Part II. and the Staff Manual respectively. Title pages will be prepared in manuscript.

Place	Date	Hour	Summary of Events and Information	Remarks and references to Appendices
ARGOEUVES	21st		W/18 H.T.M.Batty arr'd Buire. LT L. HAYBITTLE, no fruit Lieutenant. One officer 2/LT W.T. BOSTON R.F.A. and 21 O.R.s attached with battery A.O.	
	22nd		2/LT R.S. DALEY R.F.A. and three other ranks joined. Battery on gun lines	
	23rd		on Artillery training.	
	to		Battery training	
	3rd			

Signed
Commanding W/18 H.T.M.B.

Confidential

War Diary of

W/18. Heavy Trench Mortar Batt?, R.A.

from June 1st 1916 to June 30th 1916

(Volume II.)

Army Form C. 2118.

WAR DIARY
or
INTELLIGENCE SUMMARY.
(Erase heading not required.)

Volume V

Place	Date	Hour	Summary of Events and Information	Remarks and references to Appendices
Argoeuvres	June 5th		W/k H.T.M. Battery left Argoeuvres for Picquigny for Engineer fatigues.	
Picquigny	6th		Returned to Argoeuvres.	
Argoeuvres	11th		Left for Dug outs near Billon Wood.	
Billon Wood	12th		} Battery training	
"	14th			
"	14th		} Fatigues for 18th Div. Trench Mortar.	
"	15th			
"	18th		Battery lent to XIII Corps for fatigues	
Dra...	30th		Battery returned to 18th Div. Art.y No guns have yet been received by Battery	

Tom Baxter 2/Lt RFA
O.C. W/18th T.M. Battery

18/

Confidential

War-Diary of

W/18. Heavy Trench Mortar Battery. R.A.

from July 1st 1916.   to   July 31st 1916.

(Volume III.)

Volume VII.

Army Form C. 2118.

WAR DIARY
or
INTELLIGENCE SUMMARY.
(Erase heading not required.)

Instructions regarding War Diaries and Intelligence Summaries are contained in F.S. Regs., Part II. and the Staff Manual respectively. Title pages will be prepared in manuscript.

Place	Date	Hour	Summary of Events and Information	Remarks and references to Appendices
Billon Wood near Bray.	July 1st		Battery in dug-outs, Billon Wood near Bray.	
"	"		Half of the battery assisted C/51. Field Battery to take up ammunition to forward gun, and also to dig position in lines formerly occupied by the enemy in front of Carnoy under 2/Lt. W.J. Boston. Three gunners were wounded, one subsequently dying from his wounds.	
"	July 2nd-18th		Battery digging gun-positions for 18th Divisional Field Batteries.	
"	July 18th		Capt. F. Mayfield assumed command of V/18th J.M.Batty and 2/Lt. W.J. Boston assumed command of this battery.	
"	July 19th		Battery marched from Billon-Wood to No II. Section 18th D.A.C., Bray-Albert Road, near Meaulle.	
Meaulle	July 19-22nd		Fatigues for 18th Divl. Ammunition Dump.	
	July 23rd		Battery proceeded by lorries to Erondelle.	
Erondelle	July 23rd-25th		Battery Training.	
	July 26th		Battery marched to Pont-Remy.	
Pont-Remy	July 26th-27th		Fatigues for entraining 18th Divl. Art. at Pont-Remy.	
"	July 27th		Battery entrained at Pont-Remy.	
"	July 28th		Battery detrained at Bailleul and marched to Eecke.	
Eecke	July 29th-31st		Battery Training.	

Page 1.

Volume III.

Army Form C. 2118.

WAR DIARY
or
INTELLIGENCE SUMMARY.
(Erase heading not required.)

Instructions regarding War Diaries and Intelligence Summaries are contained in F. S. Regs., Part II. and the Staff Manual respectively. Title pages will be prepared in manuscript.

Place	Date	Hour	Summary of Events and Information	Remarks and references to Appendices
Eecke.	July 30th		Battery inspected by C.R.A. 18th Divn. No guns have yet been received by this battery.	

W/18 HEAVY TRENCH
MORTAR BATTERY,
R. A.

Copy.

Confidential

War-Diary

of

W/18 Heavy French Mortar Battery R.A.

from July 1st 1916   to July 31st 1916.

(Volume III)

WAR DIARY

INTELLIGENCE SUMMARY

Army Form C. 2118.

COPY

Place	Date	Hour	Summary of Events and Information	Remarks and references to Appendices
	JULY			
BILLON WOOD NEAR BRAY	1st		Battery in dug-outs. BILLON WOOD NEAR BRAY. Staff the battery assisted C/57 FIELD BATTERY to take up ammunition to forward gun and also to dig a position in line formerly occupied by the enemy in front of CARNOY under 2/LT. W.T. BOSTON. Three gunners were wounded, one subsequently dying from his wounds.	1/7/16
do.	1-18		Battery digging gun positions for 18th Divl. Field Batteries.	2/7/16
do.	18th		CAPT. L. HAYBITTEL assumed command of W/18 H.T.M. BATTY. and 2/LT. W.T. BOSTON assumed command of W/18 H.T.M. BATTY.	18/7/16
NEAR MEAULTE	19th		Battery marched to No. II. SECTION 18th DAC. BRAY–ALBERT Rd. near MEAULTE.	19/7/16
"	19th-22nd		Fatigues for 18th DIVL AMMUNITION DUMP.	19/7/16
"	23rd		Battery proceeded by lorries to ERONDELLE	23/7/16
ERONDELLE	23-25		Battery training.	25/7/16

COPY

Army Form C. 2118.

WAR DIARY
or
INTELLIGENCE SUMMARY.
(Erase heading not required.)

Place	Date	Hour	Summary of Events and Information	Remarks and references to Appendices
PONT-REMY.	July 26th-27th		Fatigues for entraining 18th DIVl ARTILLERY at PONT-REMY.	
"	27th		Battery entrained at PONT-REMY.	
BAILLEUL	28th		Battery detrained at BAILLEUL and marched to EECKE	
EECKE	29th-31st		Battery training.	
"	30th		Battery inspected by C.R.A. 18th DIVN.	
			No guns have yet been received by this battery.	

for H. Baster /A R.F.A.
O.C. W/8 H.T.M. Batt. R.A.

Confidential

War Diary

of

No 18 Heavy Trench Mortar Batty R.A.

from August 1st 1916 to August 31st 1916

(Volume IV.)

VOL.IV

Army Form C. 2118.

WAR DIARY
or
INTELLIGENCE SUMMARY.
(Erase heading not required.)

Instructions regarding War Diaries and Intelligence Summaries are contained in F.S. Regs., Part II. and the Staff Manual respectively. Title pages will be prepared in manuscript.

Place	Date	Hour	Summary of Events and Information	Remarks and references to Appendices
EECKE	Aug 1-2		Battery training	
	3rd		Battery proceeded by lorry to LE KIRLEM	
LE KIRLEM	4-8th		Battery training	
"	8th		The Battery proceeded by lorries to ERQUINGHEM-LYS.	
ERQUINGHEM -LYS	9th-24th		Half the Battery were engaged in preparing position for Heavy Trench Mortar, and half for Medium Trench Mortars.	
"	11th		CAPT. L. HAYBITTEL posted from V/18 H.T.M. Battery to V/18 H.T.M. Battery.	
"	25th		Battery marched to LE KIRLEM	
LE KIRLEM	25-29th		Battery training	

VOL. IV

Army Form C. 2118.

WAR DIARY
INTELLIGENCE SUMMARY.
(Erase heading not required.)

Instructions regarding War Diaries and Intelligence Summaries are contained in F. S. Regs., Part II. and the Staff Manual respectively. Title pages will be prepared in manuscript.

Place	Date	Hour	Summary of Events and Information	Remarks and references to Appendices
LE KIRLEM	August 29th		Battery marched to BAILLEUL and entrained for DOULLENS	MP
DOULLENS	29th 30th		Battery remaining at DOULLENS in fields	MP
"	31st		The Battery proceeded by motor lorries from DOULLENS to ALBERT.	MP

for Rooty /Lt RFA
o/c

W/18 HEAVY TRENCH
MORTAR BATTERY,
R.A.

Vol 2

Confidential

War Diary of

W/18 Heavy Trench Mortar Battery. RA

from September 1st. 1916. to September 30th 1916.

(Volume. V)

Army Form C. 2118.

WAR DIARY
~~INTELLIGENCE~~ SUMMARY
(Erase heading not required.)

Instructions regarding War Diaries and Intelligence Summaries are contained in F. S. Regs., Part II. and the Staff Manual respectively. Title pages will be prepared in manuscript.

Place	Date	Hour	Summary of Events and Information	Remarks and references to Appendices
	SEPTEMBER			
ALBERT	1-11		Battery Training	1MR.
"	11-19		The Battery was engaged in digging positions for 18th Divl. Field Batteries.	2MR.
"	20-24		Battery Training	3MR.
"	24-25		The Battery engaged in digging forward positions for 84th BDE. Field Batteries.	4MR.
"	26-29		Ten N.C.O.s and men engaged in digging positions for 84th BDE. Field Batteries	5MR.
"	30		Battery Training	6MR.

W/78 HEAVY TRENCH MORTAR BATTERY, R.A.

Confidential.

War Diary of

W/18 Heavy Trench Mortar Battery

from October 1st 1916 to October 31st 1916.

(Volume VI.)

Army Form C. 2118.

WAR DIARY
INTELLIGENCE SUMMARY.
(Erase heading not required.)

Place	Date	Hour	Summary of Events and Information	Remarks and references to Appendices
	OCTOBER 1916			
ALBERT.	1st		Battery training	[initials]
"	2nd-9th		Half the battery was engaged in digging positions for 82nd and 84th Bdes. R.F.A.	[initials]
"	9th		The battery moves into dug-outs, near CRUCIFIX CORNER, AVELUY.	[initials]
AVELUY.	9th-31st		Fatigue parties supplied for 82nd and 84th Bdes. R.F.A. Battery training	[initials]
"	28th		2/LT. W.T. BOSTON and five other ranks proceeded to IVth Army Trench Mortar School	[initials]

[signature] Lt. R.F.A.

O.C. W/18 HEAVY TRENCH MORTAR BATTERY. R.A.

War Diary
for
November 1916

X/18 M.T.M.Bty

September
18
Vol 3

WAR DIARY
or
INTELLIGENCE SUMMARY

Army Form C. 2118

Place	Date	Hour	Summary of Events and Information	Remarks and references to Appendices
St Pol & Albert	7 September		Battery out of action.	
St Pol	Sep 18th		Battery fired 20 Krupp rounds to test Williams Bar. During the work, special attention was directed to testing the loading, Sun-drive, Spindles and Rifle-barrel.	

K.S. Wesley
O.C. X 18 T.M.B., R.A.

Army Form C. 2118.

WAR DIARY
or
INTELLIGENCE SUMMARY
(Erase heading not required.)

Instructions regarding War Diaries and Intelligence Summaries are contained in F. S. Regs., Part II. and the Staff Manual respectively. Title pages will be prepared in manuscript.

Place	Date	Hour	Summary of Events and Information	Remarks and references to Appendices
Aluincourt	16th	11 A.m.	Battery moved to Albert. Men billetted in Rue de Bécourt.	
Albert	17th	9.30	Battery on wood-cutting fatigue for R.E. in Aveluy Wood.	3 Gunners to I.O.M. for repair
"	18th	"	" " " " " " "	" " " "
"	19th	"	" " " " " " "	" " " "
"	20th	"	" " " " " " "	" " " "
"	21st	"	" " " " " " "	" " " "
"	22nd	10 A.m.	Bathing parade.	
"	23rd	9.50	Battery on wood-cutting fatigue for R.E. in Aveluy Wood	
"	24th	"	" " " " " " " "	
"	25th	"	" " " " " " " "	
"	26th	"	" " " " " " " "	
"	27th	"	Inspection of Guns, and Battery Stores, by D.T.M.O.	
"	28th	10 A.m.	Guns and accessories cleaned. Inspection of Rifles and smoke helmets	
"	29th	10 "	Inspection of Rifles & equipment, and General Fatigues	
"	30th	10 "	Inspection of Rifles & equipment and General Fatigues.	

J. Ramsay
Capt.
for O.C. X/16 T.M.B.

Army Form C. 2118.

WAR DIARY
or
INTELLIGENCE SUMMARY.
(Erase heading not required.)

X 18 T.M.B., R.A.

Instructions regarding War Diaries and Intelligence Summaries are contained in F. S. Regs., Part II. and the Staff Manual respectively. Title pages will be prepared in manuscript.

October

Place	Date	Hour	Summary of Events and Information	Remarks and references to Appendices
			Reference Map. Vlieterne 57D N.E. Scale 1:10,000.	
	Oct 1st		Battery moved into action and patrons were commenced in Knox St.	
	Oct 6th	11 am	Battery commenced firing from two complete positions in Knox St. 1st rounds was "premature" which blew up gun pit. No. 2 rounds fired gauns blown up again during the night by S.O. One firing the 2nd gun the Breu Mechanism blew out after firing two rounds. 2 men wounded. (steel-shock)	
	Oct 7th		30 rounds fired	
	" 8th		47 rounds fired	
	" 9-10		New position was started in Cleared St. Vlieterne. Shelled with gas shells	
	12th		20 rounds fired - case cut in enemy hot fire zone N 23.65.2. Enemy Artillery ammunition were active.	
	13th		80 rounds fired - Observation impossible owing to glare haze of firing. Enemy had an active and Cleared St. position damaged owing to their fire.	

2353 Wt. W2544/1454 700,000 5/15 D. D. & L. A.D.S.S./Forms/C. 2118.

Army Form C. 2118.

WAR DIARY
or
INTELLIGENCE SUMMARY.
(Erase heading not required.)

Instructions regarding War Diaries and Intelligence
Summaries are contained in F. S. Regs., Part II.
and the Staff Manual respectively. Title pages
will be prepared in manuscript.

Place	Date	Hour	Summary of Events and Information	Remarks and references to Appendices
	Oct 16		No firing. Enemy Mortars & Artillery active.	
	17th	11 AM	27 rounds fires. 3rd position started in trench 81.	
	18th	11 AM	20 rounds fired. — wire cut at K.23.b.55.20 & position completed in trench 81.	
	21st	10 AM	60 rounds fired and lines cut at N.23.b.55.25, K.23.b.55.40. Owing to rain the sides of gun pit fell in and buried a gun (Chavers 81).	
	22nd		30 rounds expended, wire cut at K.23.b.55.35. One position blown up by S-9. Position repaired during the afternoon. (Chavers 81)	
	23rd		76 rounds fired — line cut at N.23.b.40.65. Chavers 81 evacuated owing to continued heavy firing by Enemy Mortars. 1 man wounded in trench.	
		2 PM		
	24th		70 rounds fired. wire cut K.23.b.55. One gun-bed was broken.	
	25th	11 AM	3 rounds fires gun pit in trench 81 blown up by Minenwerfer. Were withdrawn from 3rd position owing to very heavy shelling with 5-9 and gas shells.	
	26th	7 PM	16 rounds fired. During the new total bomb there was no retaliation. Billets in Hebuterne were shelled with gas shells. 1 man suffering from gas poisoning.	

Army Form C. 2118.

WAR DIARY
or
INTELLIGENCE SUMMARY.
(Erase heading not required.)

Instructions regarding War Diaries and Intelligence Summaries are contained in F. S. Regs., Part II. and the Staff Manual respectively. Title pages will be prepared in manuscript.

Place	Date	Hour	Summary of Events and Information	Remarks and references to Appendices
	27th	5pm	1 gun burst tires and enemy retaliated with 5.9 and gas shells. Both guns were put out of action. One gun had inter mechanism broken & in the gun. 9 men suffering from gas poison	
	28 "		Battery moved guns to Vétheune.	
	29.		Battery moved back to Crevecoeur.	
	30·31		Battery was employed in cleaning guns and making up any deficiencies in gun-teams.	

B.S. Weens Pt.
O.C. X.18 T.M.R.

Confidential
War Diary of
"X".5 Trench Mortar Battery

From December 1st 1916 to December 31st 1916.
(Volume VI)

Army Form C. 2118.

WAR DIARY
or
INTELLIGENCE SUMMARY.
(Erase heading not required.)

Place	Date	Hour	Summary of Events and Information	Remarks and references to Appendices
PETIT-PORT	17th Dec		Church parade 10 A.m. at Pont-le-Grand.	
	18th	9 a.m.	Battery on Fatigues for 82nd Bde.	
	19th	10 a.m.	T.M. Sports. to choose entries for Divisional Sports.	
	20th	9 a.m.	Battery on Fatigue for 82nd Bde. Revolver practice for N.C.O's	
	21st	"	" " " " "	
	22	"	" " " " Marching drill under B.S.M 64th Bde.	
	23rd	"	" " " " "	
	24th	"	" " " " "	
	25th		Church parade at 10 a.m at Pont-le-Grande	
			Xmas Day. Battery has Xmas dinner.	
	26th	9 a.m	Fatigues for 82nd Bde R.F.A	
	27th	"	" " " "	
	28th	"	Battery stores moved to Abbeville by lorry and men marched	
	29th	"	Battery entrained for Acheux and arrived 10 p.m.	
	30th	"	Stores moved to 61st D.A.C Camp by wagons and men marched - tents pitched in very muddy place	
	31st	"	Battery on fatigues loading lorries with Nisson huts for H.Q 10th R.A	

WAR DIARY
INTELLIGENCE SUMMARY

Army Form C. 2118.

X 18 T.M.B. R.A.

December

Place	Date	Hour	Summary of Events and Information	Remarks and references to Appendices
ALBERT	Dec 1	9.30	Inspection of Rifles and General Fatigues.	
"	" 2	"	" " " "	
"	" 3	"	" " " "	
PETIT PORT	" 4		Battery moves by lorries to Petit-Port.	
"	" 5	9.30	Inspection & General Fatigue.	
"	" 6	9 p.m.	Battery on fatigue making horse troughs & swing pits	
"	" 7	"	" " " " "	
"	" 8	"	" " " " "	
"	" 9	9.30	Gun drill + Rifle Drill	
"	" 10	10 p.m.	Church Parade at Pont-a-Grandes	
"	" 11	"	Inspection and General Fatigue	
"	" 12	2 p.m.	Marching Drill by R.S.M. 64th Bde.	
"	" 13	9.30	Inspection and General Fatigues	
"	" 14		" "	
"	15	9 a.m.	Battery on fatigues for 82nd Bde & marching drill with R.S.M. 84 + Bde	
	16		Fatigues for 82nd Bde.	

Army Form C. 2118.

WAR DIARY
or
INTELLIGENCE SUMMARY
(Erase heading not required.)

X 1st T.M.B. R.A.

Instructions regarding War Diaries and Intelligence Summaries are contained in F.S. Regs., Part II and the Staff Manual respectively. Title pages will be prepared in manuscript.

Place	Date	Hour	Summary of Events and Information	Remarks and references to Appendices
Rim Camp	Nov 1st		Guns and all accessories cleaned and overhauled.	
"	" 2nd		Rifles and smoke helmets inspected	
"	" 3rd		Men were issued with two blankets each.	
"	" 4th		Gun cleaning & practical instruction in horse care with dummy signalling	
"	" 5th		Kit inspection. Any deficiencies were indented for.	
"	" 6th		Rifle drill and squelching	
"	" 7th		Bathing Parade	
"	" 8th		—	
"	" 9th		Gun cleaning and overhauling	
"	" 10th		" "	
"	" 11th		All men were employed by 21st bn on fatigues at Hihtumel	
"	" 12th		7 men required for fatigues by 31st Division.	
"	" 13th		Heavy shelling with 5-9 shells.	
"	" 14th		Gun cleaning. Wincuup lorry shield.	
"	" 15th		Gun cleaning	

Army Form C. 2118.

WAR DIARY
or
INTELLIGENCE SUMMARY.
(Erase heading not required.) X/18 T.M.B., R.A.

Place	Date	Hour	Summary of Events and Information	Remarks and references to Appendices
			JANUARY	
Bonjuiwral	Jan 1	9am	Battery on fatigues erecting Nisson huts for HQ 18th RA.	
"	2	"	"	
"	3	"	"	
"	4	"	"	
"	5	"	" pitching tents for 74th Bde R.F.A	
"	6	"	"	Sgt. Whitehead awarded D.C.M.
"	7	"	"	2 new guns complete received from D.A.P.20
"	8	"	Fatigue erecting Nisson huts & making horse lines for HQ 18th RA	
"	9	"	"	
"	10	"	As above. Corpl & 4 men sent to Aveluy to get Nisson huts for Medium TM Battys	
"	11	"	as above	
"	12th	"	as above	
Authuile Wood	13th	10am	Battery moves to Authuile Wood and tents pitched adjoining 82 Bde HQ. Stores & guns left behind in charge of Bombardier	
"	14th	9pm	Battery on fatigues building gun pits etc for 73rd Bde R.F.A	

Army Form C. 2118.

WAR DIARY
or
INTELLIGENCE SUMMARY.
(Erase heading not required.)

Instructions regarding War Diaries and Intelligence Summaries are contained in F. S. Regs., Part II. and the Staff Manual respectively. Title pages will be prepared in manuscript.

Place	Date	Hour	Summary of Events and Information	Remarks and references to Appendices
Authuille	15th	9 am	Fatigues for 83rd Bde as before.	
"	16th	"	"	After inspection
"	17th	"	"	
"	18th	"	"	
"	19th	"	" 2 men to 82"Bde to erect Baths.	
"	20th	"	"	
"	21st	"	" 4 men to 82 Bde to erect baths.	
"	22nd	"	"	
"	23rd	"	"	" 2 men to Sig Course
"	24th	"	"	
"	25th	"	" 2 " make horse lines	
"	26th	"	Fatigues for 84th Bde RFA and 2 "	
"	27th	"	"	
"	28th	"	"	
"	29th	"	Fatigues for 83rd Bde RFA	
"	30th	"	" 84th Bde RFA	
"	31st	"	"	

E. Westwood
OC X/16 TMB RA

Army Form C. 2118.

WAR DIARY
or
INTELLIGENCE SUMMARY.
(Erase heading not required.)

X 18TH B RA FEBRUARY

Instructions regarding War Diaries and Intelligence Summaries are contained in F.S. Regs., Part II. and the Staff Manual respectively. Title pages will be prepared in manuscript.

Place	Date	Hour	Summary of Events and Information	Remarks and references to Appendices
Caulkule Wood	Feb 1	8.30am	Men on fatigues - building gun-pits for 84th Brigade RFA	
	2		" " "	
	3		" " "	
	4		" " " Rifle Inspection	
	5		" " "	
	6		" " for 83rd Bde. Corpl Sullivan Fofes with Hq 1st Rue RTC	
	7		fatigues as before	
	8		" " 2 men sent to School of hussars.	
	9		Men on fatigues for 84th Bde RFA	
	10		" "	
	11		" "	
	12		" "	
	13		" "	
	14		" "	
	15		" "	
	16		" "	

WAR DIARY or INTELLIGENCE SUMMARY.

Army Form C. 2118.

Place	Date	Hour	Summary of Events and Information	Remarks and references to Appendices
Continued	Feb/17		Men on fatigue for O.C. Batte RGA	
	18		" " " 53" Batt RGA	
	19		" " " " "	
	20		" " " 74th Batt RGA	
	21		" " " " " Reserve rations consumed	
	22		" " " " " Inspection of Gun Relieves	
	23		" " " " "	
	24		" " " Sct C/84 and 5 ct A/84 Paid men	
	25		Men were kept in readiness in case they were required	
	26		Fatigues for 82nd Batte RGA	
	27		" " " 74 Batte RGA	
	28		Men on fatigues at breeches gun pits of 162nd Batte loading up ammunition	

B.R. Walsh Lt
OC XISTMB RA

WAR DIARY or INTELLIGENCE SUMMARY.

Army Form C. 2118.

X 18 T.M.B. R.A

MARCH

Reference map: - ARRAS

Place	Date	Hour	Summary of Events and Information	Remarks and references to Appendices
Aubigny Wood	1st	8.30am	Men on fatigue for 8th Bde watering ammunition. Paraded again at 9.30pm and worked during night near Wood of 18th bn Amm. Officer	
"	2		No parades	
"	3		Men on fatigue watering ammunition at 8.30am and 5pm.	
"	4		Rifle inspection	
"	5	8.30am	Ammunition fatigues	
"	6		" "	
"	7		" "	
"	8		Battery moved by horses and arrived at AUBIGNY.	
AUBIGNY	9	9am	Inspection of Battery	
"	10	4pm	Battery moved by lorries and arrived at ARRAS.	
ARRAS	11	10am	2 completed to incomplete position taken over from 9th bn T.M.	
			2 guns were ready to fire at night. Battery sector Q.18.a 4.3 to River cut at Q.18 & 25.60. Enemy troops	
	17	noon	15 rounds fired and line cut at Q.18 & 25.60. Enemy troops mechanism jammed on other gun.	
		5.30	26 rounds fired and gaps cut in enemy wire at Q.18.c 3.9	

WAR DIARY or INTELLIGENCE SUMMARY.

(Erase heading not required.)

Army Form C. 2118.

Place	Date	Hour	Summary of Events and Information	Remarks and references to Appendices
ARRAS	13th	2pm	40 minnits fired - one gap 20 yds wide cut at q.18.a.3.0. Gaps 5x wide cut at q.18.c.3.0.95 + q.18.c.30.87. Some wire damaged at q.18.c.25.70. Enemy retaliates with heavy minenwerfer.	
"	14th	1pm	Rounds fired 30. Small gap cut at q.18.c.7. Gap 5x wide at q.18.c.3.9. Enemy retaliated on one gun pit with whizz-bangs.	
"	15th	2pm	38 rounds fires Gaps 5x wide at q.18.c.25.55 + q.18.c.20.46. Some wire damaged at q.18.c.30.93. Enemy retaliates with whizz bangs.	
"	16th	1pm	Rounds fires 38. Gaps cut 5x wide at q.18.c.2.6 + q.18.c.2.8. Enemy retaliated with intense fire from heavy minenwerfer. 6 rounds apis were fired at Brigades posten of minenwerfer and trench crews.	
"	17th	1.30pm	Rounds fires 53. Gap 10x wide cut at q.18.c.2.5. Gaps 5x wide cut at q.18.c.23.73. Enemy retaliation nil.	
"	18th	2pm	Rounds fires 52. Gap cut 10x wide at q.18.c.25.65. Wire damages at q.18.a.30.02. Enemy retaliation nil. During the evening enemy team up two gun-pits at q.17.a.5.6 by minenwerfer thereby rendering them useless.	

Army Form C. 2118.

WAR DIARY
or
INTELLIGENCE SUMMARY.
(Erase heading not required.)

Instructions regarding War Diaries and Intelligence Summaries are contained in F.S. Regs., Part II. and the Staff Manual respectively. Title pages will be prepared in manuscript.

Place	Date	Hour	Summary of Events and Information	Remarks and references to Appendices
ARRAS	19th	4pm	Rounds fired 48. 13 duds owing to strong wind which prevented front from causing headcon. Gap cut 10x wide 9.18.c.25.73.	
	20th		Rounds fired 65. Sap 10x wide at 9.18.c.25.73. Some damages on 9.18.c.25.63. Enemy retaliates with intense fire from heavy minenwerfers.	
	21st		Rounds fired 45. Sap 10x wide at 9.18.A.3.1. Retaliation from minenwerfer & 10.5 cm gun.	
	22nd		Rounds fired 82. 4 small gaps between 9.18.A.30.05 & 9.18.A.4.15 am guns.	
	23rd		Rounds fired 100. Gap 10x wide at 9.18.A.4.3. & 5x wide at 9.18.A.30.15. Retaliation from 10.5 cm. 9.15 am guns. Retaliation NIL	
	24th		Rounds fired 100. Wire much damaged on this front. Retaliation NIL	
	25th		Rounds fires 50. Retaliation with 10.5 cm shells.	
	26th		Rounds fired 80. Retaliation with 10.5 cm shells.	
	27th		Rounds fired 50. Gap cut at 9.18.A.35.15. Retaliation NIL	
	28th		Rounds fired 50. 2 gun pits blown up owing to heavy accur. by 10.5 + 15 cm.	
	29th		Rounds fired 50. Wire damaged at 9.18.c.25.95.	
	30		Men on fatigues repairing damaged parties. No firing	
	31st		Rounds fires 50. Total rounds fires during month 1034.	

A.F. M/M DB OA
OC × 18 TAB OA

Army Form C. 2118.

WAR DIARY
or
INTELLIGENCE SUMMARY.
(Erase heading not required.)

Instructions regarding War Diaries and Intelligence Summaries are contained in F. S. Regs., Part II. and the Staff Manual respectively. Title pages will be prepared in manuscript.

Place	Date	Hour	Summary of Events and Information	Remarks and references to Appendices
ARRAS	9th		Guns moved out of action & men returned to billets in ARRAS	
	10th		Guns & stores cleaned and overhauled. Deficiencies indents for.	
	11th	9am	Inspection of guns	
	12th	9am	Rifle Inspection.	
	13th	9am	Men paraded for pay	
	14th	9.30	Inspection of men returns equipment	
	15th	"	Gun cleaning & general fatigues.	
	16th	"	"	
	17th	"	Inspection of kit and rifle drill.	
	18th	"	Gun cleaning.	
	19th	"	Parade & inspection	
	20th	"	"	
	21st	"	Gun cleaning & general fatigue	
	22nd	"	Gun cleaning & general fatigues	
	23rd	"	Kit inspection.	
	24th	"	Rifle Drill	

Army Form C. 2118.

WAR DIARY
or
INTELLIGENCE SUMMARY.
(Erase heading not required.)

X 181 T.M.B. R.A.   April

Instructions regarding War Diaries and Intelligence Summaries are contained in F.S. Regs., Part II. and the Staff Manual respectively. Title pages will be prepared in manuscript.

Place	Date	Hour	Summary of Events and Information	Remarks and references to Appendices
ARRAS			Reference map ARRAS	
	1st	12 noon	Rounds fired 50. One gun pit blown in	
	2nd	1 pm	Rounds fired 50. One mechanism blown out.	
	3rd	—	No firing. All men turned to repairing positions.	
	4th	9–10 am	"V" Bay. 250 rounds fired on enemy wire. Battery moved up into trenches.	
		2–4 pm	"W" Bay. 250 rounds fired on enemy wire. Retaliation from 15cm shell.	
	5th	11–12 pm	"X" Bay. Enemy retaliates with 10.5 + 15 cm shells. Special attention paid to	
		4.45 pm	wire in front of Sap V2. One gun out of action owing to	
	6th	9–10 am	"Y" Bay. 240 rounds fired. broken trunnion frame. One gun pit blown up.	
		2–4 pm	"Z" Bay. 250 rounds fired on enemy wire. One gun pit blown in	
	7th	11–1 pm	"X" & "Y" Bay. Retaliation from 15 cm shells on shell landing in	
		4.45 pm	Heavy retaliation from 15 cm shells on gun pit. Fires to explode.	
	8th	11–1 pm	"Y" Bay. 240 rounds fired on enemy front line. Special attention paid to Sap V2 & M.G. emplacements at G.15a v.v. Retaliation	
		4.45 pm	from 10.5cm + 15 cm shells.	
	9th		"Z" Bay. Zero hour 5·30 A.m. One round fired at Zero hour on enemy front line, then rapid fire for 3 mins on support line	

Army Form C. 2118.

WAR DIARY
or
INTELLIGENCE SUMMARY.
(Erase heading not required.)

Instructions regarding War Diaries and Intelligence Summaries are contained in F. S. Regs., Part II. and the Staff Manual respectively. Title pages will be prepared in manuscript.

Place	Date	Hour	Summary of Events and Information	Remarks and references to Appendices
ARRAS	25th		Gun cleaning + general fatigues	
	26		"	
	27		Battery inspection gun drill	
	28		Battery moves to Blangy/sum to join 81st Bde: moves - Wub forms at Penin.	
	29th		Battery moves from Penin + goes into Bitty at Beauvains	
Beauvains	30th		General fatigues	

Army Form C. 2118.

WAR DIARY
or
INTELLIGENCE SUMMARY.   X187 T.M.B. R.A
(Erase heading not required.)

MAY

Instructions regarding War Diaries and Intelligence Summaries are contained in F. S. Regs., Part II. and the Staff Manual respectively. Title pages will be prepared in manuscript.

Place	Date	Hour	Summary of Events and Information	Remarks and references to Appendices
BEAURAINS	1st	9am	Gun drill and Rifle drill.	
"	2nd	"	Gun cleaning and General fatigues.	
"	3rd	"	Semaphore and instruction. Reprimers indented for.	
"	4th	"	Marching drill and revolver practice.	
"	5th	"	Gun drill.	
"	6th	"	Gun cleaning & fatigues.	
"	7th	"	Camp fatigues	
"	8th	"	Rifle drill.	
"	9th	"	Inspection & gun drill	
"	10th	"	Gun cleaning	
"	11th	"	Semaphore instruction	
"	12th	"	Semaphore "	
"	13th	"	Lecture on telephone	
"	14th	"	Gun cleaning	
"	15th	"	" "	
"	16th	"	General fatigues.	

Army Form C. 2118.

WAR DIARY
or
INTELLIGENCE SUMMARY.
(Erase heading not required.)

Instructions regarding War Diaries and Intelligence Summaries are contained in F. S. Regs., Part II. and the Staff Manual respectively. Title pages will be prepared in manuscript.

Place	Date	Hour	Summary of Events and Information	Remarks and references to Appendices
BEAURAINS	17th	9 p.m.	Fatigues and marching drill.	
"	18th	"	Physical training	
St Martin sur Cojeul	19th	"	Battery moved to St Martin sur Cojeul - Guns left at Beaurains	
"	20th	"	Battery on fatigues for D/163. digging gun-pits and dug outs	
"	do	"	working from 9 a.m to 3 p.m	
"	29th			
"	30 to 31		Battery on fatigues for D/162. digging gun-pits and dug outs	

B. Wilson
Lt
2nd Lieut R.A.
O.C. 182nd B

Army Form C. 2118.

WAR DIARY
or
INTELLIGENCE SUMMARY.
(Erase heading not required.)

June 1917

X/18 T.M.B. R.A.

Place	Date	Hour	Summary of Events and Information	Remarks and references to Appendices
St Martin aux-Cojeul	1st	8.30	Battery on fatigue for various field batteries - digging Gun-pits etc.	
"	do	"	Inspection and marching drill	
"	23rd	"	"	
"	24th	"	Instruction in use of Box respirators.	
"	25th	"	Semaphore + inspection.	
"	26th	"		
Henderson	27th	9am	Battery moving to A.T.N. into camp near Henderson.	
"	28th	9am	"	
"	29th	"	On fatigues preparing Sports Ground	
"	30th	"	"	

K S Mearns Lt
OC X 18 T.M.B. R.A.

Army Form C. 2118.

WAR DIARY
or
INTELLIGENCE SUMMARY.
(Erase heading not required.)

Place	Date	Hour	Summary of Events and Information	Remarks and references to Appendices
BEAURAINS	7th	9 am	Fatigues and marching drill.	
"	18th		Physical training	
Marlin en cigne	19th		Battery moved to St Martin sur-Cojeul – guns left at Beaurains	
"	20th to 29th		Battery on fatigues for D/163. digging gun - pits and dug outs working from 9 am to 3 pm.	
"	30 to 31		Battery on fatigues for D/162. digging gun pits and dug outs.	

B.F. Weller?
O.C. 168th R B R.A.

Army Form C. 2118.

WAR DIARY
or
INTELLIGENCE SUMMARY.
(Erase heading not required.)

X 18 T.M.B. R.A.   June 1917

Place	Date	Hour	Summary of Events and Information	Remarks and references to Appendices
St Martin au Cojeul	1st	8.30	Battery on fatigues for various field batteries – digging gun-pits etc.	
"	do	"	"	
"	23rd	"	Inspection and marching drill.	
"	24th	"	Instruction in use of box respirators.	
"	25th	"	"	
"	26th	"	Semaphore & inspection.	
Henducourt	27th	9am	Battery move to A.T.N. rest camp near Henducourt	
"	28th	9am	" on fatigues preparing sports ground	
"	29th	"	"	
"	30th	"	"	

K.S. Wead(?) 2/Lt
O/C x 18 T.M.B. R.A.

Army Form C. 2118.

WAR DIARY
or
INTELLIGENCE SUMMARY.
(Erase heading not required.)

July 1917 X18 TMB. RA.

Instructions regarding War Diaries and Intelligence Summaries are contained in F.S. Regs., Part II. and the Staff Manual respectively. Title pages will be prepared in manuscript.

Place	Date	Hour	Summary of Events and Information	Remarks and references to Appendices
Thieushouck	July 1st	9am	Battery on fatigues preparing Sports Ground.	
"	2nd	"	Bn Ath. Sports	
"	3rd	"	Battery moves by lorries to Koulleur & billets there.	
Poulleur	4th	2pm	Battery entrained & arrived at Godewaersvelde - detrained and marched to billets at Steenwoorde. (map Hazebrouck 15A)	
Steenwoorde	5th		General fatigues.	
"	6th		Gun cleaning + marching drill.	
"	7th		Inspection and rifle drill	
"	8th		Gun cleaning and general fatigues.	
"	9th		Marching drill.	
"	10th		Box respirator drill.	
"	11th		"	
DICKEBUSCH	12th		Battery moved by lorry to Hut in Dickebusch Area.	
"	13th		1 NCO + 3 men part to dump +5 men on fatigues for O/83.	
"	14th		Gun cleaning.	
"	15th		Men returned from dump.	

Army Form C. 2118.

WAR DIARY
or
INTELLIGENCE SUMMARY.
(Erase heading not required.)

Instructions regarding War Diaries and Intelligence Summaries are contained in F. S. Regs., Part II. and the Staff Manual respectively. Title pages will be prepared in manuscript.

Place	Date	Hour	Summary of Events and Information	Remarks and references to Appendices
DICKEBUSCH	16th	9 am	Gun cleaning & general fatigues. Men returned from D/83	
"	17th	"	Inspection and gun drill	
"	18th	"	Gun inspection drill.	
"	19th	"	Gun cleaning general fatigue.	
"	20	"	Box inspection drill	
"	21	"	Kit inspection.	
"	22	"	Gun cleaning general fatigues.	
"	23	"	Gun drill & semaphore	
"	24	"	General fatigue	
"	25	"	Parade and inspection	
"	26	"	Gun cleaning	
"	27	8 pm	Fatigues on dump.	
"	28	"	Fatigues on dump.	
"	29	6 pm	Battery on fatigue putting up dump at Chateen Segard	
"	30	1 pm	Parade & inspection	
"	31	7 am	Battery stood by as reserve stretcher - bearers.	

K F Nellis Y
O C X18 TMB

Army Form C. 2118.

WAR DIARY
or
INTELLIGENCE SUMMARY.

(Erase heading not required.)   X/18 T.M.B. R.A.   August 1917

Instructions regarding War Diaries and Intelligence Summaries are contained in F. S. Regs., Part II. and the Staff Manual respectively. Title pages will be prepared in manuscript.

Place	Date	Hour	Summary of Events and Information	Remarks and references to Appendices
DICKEBUSCH	1st	6.27a	Three N.C.Os. Gunners attached to A/82 for trade	
"	1st	6.27p	Two N.C.Os. " " " B/82 " "	
"	2nd		Lieut (now Capt) D.C. Meadus posted to and assumed command of V/18 H.T.M.B.	
"	2nd		Lieut (now Lieut) R.H. McLenchlin assumed command of X/18 T.M.B. vice "Meadus" transferred	
"	28		Nine N.C.Os + men attached to A/82 for trade	
"	24		" " " B/82 " "	
"	29		do - do - do	
"	30		Two N.C.Os. + men	
"	30		Battery moved by lorries to fresh area at OUDEZEELE (Map Hazebrouck 5A)	
OUDEZEELE	30		Two N.C.Os. + men returned from B/82	
"	31		Gun cleaning and general fatigues	

B. McLenchlin
Lt. R.A.
O.C. X/18 T.M.B. R.A.

Army Form C. 2118.

WAR DIARY
~~INTELLIGENCE SUMMARY~~
(Erase heading not required.)

A/9 ~~LL~~ B Bde September 1917

Place	Date	Hour	Summary of Events and Information	Remarks and references to Appendices
OUDEZEELE	1st		Nine N.C.Os and men joined from A/63 Brigade. R.F.A.	
"	2nd		Parades and inspection.	
"	3rd		G.O.C. I Corps inspected the Divisional Artillery and Personnel awards	
"	4th		Semaphore and Gun Cleaning.	
"	5th		Gun Drill	
"	6th		Gun Drill General Fatigues	
"	7th		Inspection of Rifles and Smoke Helmets — marching drill.	
"	8th		Under arrangements made by D.N. Arty the battery spent to-day at the Seaside near Dunkerque	
"	9th		Church Parade.	
"	10th		Inspection of Horn Rations and Smoke Helmet drill.	
"	11th		Gun Drill	
"	12th		Lectures — Marching Drill.	
"	13th		Inspection of Rifles and Gun Cleaning	
"	14th		Gun Drill	
"	15th		Musketry Physical drill.	
"	16th		Church Parade.	

Army Form C. 2118.

WAR DIARY
or
INTELLIGENCE SUMMARY. 4/87 T.M.B. R.A. September 1917
(Erase heading not required.)

Instructions regarding War Diaries and Intelligence Summaries are contained in F. S. Regs., Part II. and the Staff Manual respectively. Title pages will be prepared in manuscript.

Place	Date	Hour	Summary of Events and Information	Remarks and references to Appendices
OUDEZEELE	18th		Gun Cleaning	
"	19th		Inspection Smoke helmet drill	
"	19th		Inspection of two Rifles and fuse charts	
"	20th		Battery moved by lorries to their new camp at SERQUES (Map Hazebrouck 5A)	
SERQUES	21st		Smoke helmet drill and Semaphore	
"	22nd		Rifle, Revolver and machine drills	
"	23rd		Gun Cleaning	
"	24th	10.30	Battery moved by lorries to intermediate station at ZEGGERS-CAPPEL	
ZEGGERS-CAPPEL	25th	10.40	Battery moved by lorries to forward area at POPERINGHE	
POPERINGHE	26th		Gun Cleaning. Small Arms inspection.	
"	27th		Gun & Rifle Drill. Inspection of Stores & gas apparatus.	
"	28th	3.00	Battery moved by lorries to VLAMERTINGHE took over British from 48th Div. Trench Mortar.	
VLAMERTINGHE	29th		Rifle and Revolver inspection. Gun Cleaning. Gas Helmet inspection	
"	30th		Fired A.E. Vankier R.A. Brady at TAUNTON JUNCTION. Y.O.R? for fatigue for 291. Bde. R.F.A.	

P.M.Combie.
Lieut R.F.A.
O.C. 4/18 T.M. B. R.A.

Army Form C. 2118.

X/18 J.M. Batt's

WAR DIARY
or
INTELLIGENCE SUMMARY.

(Erase heading not required.)

October 1914

Instructions regarding War Diaries and Intelligence Summaries are contained in F. S. Regs., Part II. and the Staff Manual respectively. Title pages will be prepared in manuscript.

Place	Date	Hour	Summary of Events and Information	Remarks and references to Appendices
VLAMERTINGHE	1st		4 men attached to 29½ Brigade R.F.A. on fatigue.	
"	2nd		"	
"	3rd		2 men attached to 9/3 Bde. R.F.A. on fatigue.	
"	4th		2 men rejoined from 9/3 Bde. R.F.A.	
"	5th		2 men attached to 9/3 Bde. R.F.A. for work.	
"	6th		"	
"	7th		4 men rejoined from 29½ Bde. R.F.A.	
"	8th		General fatigue – completing Splinter-proof dugouts.	
"	9th		Inspection of rifles – feetwear and marching drill. 1 N.C.O. & 3 men on fatigue at JOURNE Dump.	
"	10th		General fatigues. Guns cleaning.	
"	11th		Battery moved by G.S. wagons and took over billets from 5th D.A. at TROIS TOURS. B28 A10. (Capt Hopgood Shier, 2nd Lt Eb. b. B.)	
"	12th		1 man attached to B/85 for work. 2 men transferred from 9/5 to B/85 for rest.	
"	13th		General fatigues "gun cleaning"	
TROIS TOURS	14th		"	
"	15th		4/ Oflank tactics from 18th D.A.C.	

Army Form C. 2118.

WAR DIARY
or
INTELLIGENCE SUMMARY.

(Erase heading not required.) October 1917.

Instructions regarding War Diaries and Intelligence Summaries are contained in F. S. Regs., Part II. and the Staff Manual respectively. Title pages will be prepared in manuscript.

Place	Date	Hour	Summary of Events and Information	Remarks and references to Appendices
Trois Tours	14th		General fatigues. 10 Ranks rejoined from Base Depôt.	
"	18th		" Rifle inspection drill. Smoke helmets inspection.	
"	19th		3 men rejoined from B/83. 1 NCO & 9 men attached to C/83 for fatigue	
"	20th		1 NCO & 9 men attached to C/83 for fatigue	
"	21st		"	
"	22nd		"	
"	23rd		"	
"	24th		" 3 men rejoined from ZOUANE DUMP. 1 NCO & 9 men attached to D/83 for duty	
"	25th		" 1 NCO & 9 men attached to D/83 for duty	
"	26th		"	
"	27th		"	
"	28th		"	
"	29th		"	
"	30th		"	
"	31st		"	

J. Abercrombie Lieut 16th
OC 4/8 TorB Rn

Army Form C. 2118.

WAR DIARY of X/18 T.M. B'y

or INTELLIGENCE SUMMARY.

(Erase heading not required.) November 1916

Instructions regarding War Diaries and Intelligence Summaries are contained in F. S. Regs., Part II. and the Staff Manual respectively. Title pages will be prepared in manuscript.

Place	Date	Hour	Summary of Events and Information	Remarks and references to Appendices
Trois Tours	1st to 3rd		1 N.C.O and 9 men attached to C/83 for fatigues	
"	4th		" " " " 2 men attached to D/82 for fatigues.	
"	5th		1 man rejoined from Expedition course at D.A.C.	
"	6th		1 man attached to 6 D.A.C. for Expedition course	
"	20th		" "	
"	21st		1 N.C.O. at Louvre Dump.	
"	23rd		1 N.C.O. + 9 men Rejoined from C/83 Bde. R.F.A.	
"	29th		" men work under orders of Corps Salvage Officer.	
"	30th		" " "	2 O.C's joined from 1st 2 A.C
	30-11-16			

D. Mukonzi
Lt. RFA
OC 4/18 T.M.B. RA

Army Form C. 2118.

WAR DIARY
~~INTELLIGENCE SUMMARY.~~
(Erase heading not required.)

4/1st French Mountain Battery

December 1917.

Mesop". Sharpshooters S.A.

[signature]
Lieut RFA
OC 4/1st T.M.B. RA

Army Form C. 2118.

WAR DIARY
or
INTELLIGENCE SUMMARY. Dec 1917.

(Erase heading not required.)

Instructions regarding War Diaries and Intelligence Summaries are contained in F. S. Regs., Part II and the Staff Manual respectively. Title pages will be prepared in manuscript.

Place	Date	Hour	Summary of Events and Information	Remarks and references to Appendices
TROIS TOURS	1st		NCO & 4 men for work under Corps Salvage Officer. NCO & 20 OR DUMP. 2 men attached DR/L (10 salvage) 1 man attached to D.P.L. for operating canteen.	
	2nd		1 NCO returned from 20 O.R. Dump and attached for duties under Corps Salvage Officer.	
	11th			
	12th		2 NCOs & 7 men returned from Corps Salvage work. 2 men reported from B/82.	
	13th		Having moved to limits to use area at CHOCQUES. (Hqs Squadron at S.P.)	
ECOMBELLE	14th		Inspection. Sword of Belgium	
	15th		"	
	16th		Gun Drill. Rifle musketry drill.	
	17th		"	
	18th		Sword & lance drill.	
	19th		Cleaning. Harness. Sword drill.	
	20th		Ditto. Sword & lance drill.	
	21st		Musketry. Sword drill.	
	22nd		Smartness. Kit Inspection.	
	23rd		Church Parade.	
	24th		Gun Drill. Rifle musketry Musketry drill.	

Army Form C. 2118.

WAR DIARY
or
INTELLIGENCE SUMMARY. DEC 1917 (CONT?)
(Erase heading not required.)

Place	Date	Hour	Summary of Events and Information	Remarks and references to Appendices
COMBERS	25th		Christmas Day - Holiday. Preview Attached to D.A.C. for course of Signalling	
"	26th		General Fatigues "	
"	27th		Inspection from Divn Sub Services Dir "	
"	28th		" Cleaning. Marching & Rifle exercise drill	
"	29th		" Instruction in use of telephone & advise reconnaissance "	
"	30th		" General Parade	
"	31st		" General Fatigues preparing to move.	

31/Dec/17

[signature]
Lieut RA
O.C. 1/N Fo.L.B. R.A

Army Form C. 2118.

WAR DIARY
or
INTELLIGENCE SUMMARY.
(Erase heading not required.)

January 1918

Place	Date	Hour	Summary of Events and Information	Remarks and references to Appendices

A/18 Trench Mortar Battery R.A.

January 1918.

Reference Maps:- Sheet sheet 5.A.
Ypres, sheet 28 N.W.

January 31st 1918.

Administration
Lieut R.H.
OC A/18.T.M.B. R.A

Army Form C. 2118.

WAR DIARY
or
INTELLIGENCE SUMMARY. January 1918
(Erase heading not required.)

Instructions regarding War Diaries and Intelligence Summaries are contained in F.S. Regs., Part II. and the Staff Manual respectively. Title pages will be prepared in manuscript.

Place	Date	Hour	Summary of Events and Information	Remarks and references to Appendices
CROMBEKE	1st		Wagons moved by lorries to forward areas and took over billets of 57th Divl Train Master at LARREY CAMP (B9.C.11) Sh.28 NW (Belgium)	
LARREY CAMP (EUROPAGHE)	2nd		General Duties (men attached to D.A.C. for Signalling course)	
"	3rd		2 NCOs & 10 men proceed to STRAY FARM (C.2.C.27) to be employed on Salvage work. (Sh.u 28 NW) (Belgium)	
"	4th		"	
"	5th		"	
"	6th		"	
"			NCO attached to O.C Salvage Duty	
"	7th		and 3 ORs proceed to 2nd Army School at LOCHINGHEM for a Drill Master Course	
"	8th		3 NCOs & 10 men on Salvage work. 3 ORs to 2nd Army T.M. School. 1 man attached to D.A.C for Signalling course	
			Lieut R.R. McCombie R.F.A. proceeded to Stray Farm (C.2.C.27) to assume on Salvage work.	
"	9th&12th		3 NCOs & 10 men on Salvage work. 3 Officers & 2nd Army T.M. School. 1 man attached to D.A.C for Signalling Course	
"	13th		"	
"	14th		1 NCO & 10 O.R. joined Salvage Party at STRAY FARM.	
"	15th&14th		4 NCOs & 11 men on Salvage work	
"	19th		1 OR. sent on Course of Instruction	
"	20th		4 NCOs & 10 men on Salvage work. 3 O.R.s to RE? from 2nd Army T.M. School	

Army Form C. 2118.

WAR DIARY
or
INTELLIGENCE SUMMARY.
(Erase heading not required.)

Instructions regarding War Diaries and Intelligence Summaries are contained in F. S. Regs., Part II. and the Staff Manual respectively. Title pages will be prepared in manuscript.

Place	Date	Hour	Summary of Events and Information	Remarks and references to Appendices
LARKEY CAMP (ELVERDINGHE)	21st		4 N.C.Os & 10 men on Salvage work. 1 man in charge of wireless. 1 man attached to D.A.C. for Signalling course.	
"	22nd		" Returned to ELVERDINGHE "	Lieut. McCombie rel'd to Brigade h/q.
"	23rd		1 N.C.O & 3 men proceeded to STRAY FARM to be employed on Salvage work.	
"	"		" on Salvage work. 1 man on course of wireless. 1 man attached to D.A.C. for Signalling course.	
"	24th		Remainder NCOs & men employed daily under orders received from R.A. HQrs Division.	
"	25th		"	
"	26th		"	
"	27th		"	
"	28th		"	
"	29th		"	
"	30th		"	
"	31st		"	

31-1-18.

D. Aitchbould
Lieut R.F.A
O.C. 4/18 T.M.B R.A.

18th Div.

WAR DIARY

X/18 TRENCH MORTAR BATTERY, R.A.

M A R C H

1 9 1 8

WAR DIARY / INTELLIGENCE SUMMARY

Army Form C. 2118

X/18 Trench Mortar Battery

March 1918

Place	Date	Hour	Summary of Events and Information	Remarks and references to Appendices
REMIGNY	18		Repairing Mortar emplacements at LYFONTAINE No 5 (Map Ref L 66 c 3 w) & FORT VENDEUIL No 23.13 (Map Ref U 6 c S W 2). Bomb Repairs & Infantry Drill was carried out daily.	
	19		Emplacement completed. Mortars ready for action. Ammunition yet complete with 100 rounds.	
	19/20		Work continued on remaining Mortar emplacements	
	21	4.35 am	German attack began. Mortars at FORT VENDEUIL were not ready for action. The detachments working with Infantry until orders were given to retire to Battn position were sent under cover and were carried out under Battery Commander. Our Mortar at LYFONTAINE was ready for action but no firing was to take away to be left, that the position of our Infantry was unknown. Later in the day the Mortar was destroyed by Lieut Levi. Detachments working under orders from Battalion Commander. Orders were issued to withdraw.	
VALLEQUIER AUMONT	21/31		Personnel from LYFONTAINE attached to No 1 Section D.A.C.	

Allen, Capt.
R.F.A.

18th Div.

X/18 TRENCH MORTAR BATTERY, R.A.

A P R I L

1 9 1 8

WAR DIARY or INTELLIGENCE SUMMARY.

Army Form C. 2118.

X/R T.M.B RA

APRIL 1918

(Erase heading not required.)

Place	Date	Hour	Summary of Events and Information	Remarks and references to Appendices
Inv of Hurd	1st/7th		Battery attached to 119th section 18th D.A.C. Moving coin of road	
Charry	8th		Battery marched to Charry	
"	9th		Inspection and general fatigues	
Warlus	10th		Battery moved by march to Harlus	
Brondsart	11th		" " " " Brondsart	
"	12th/14th		Parades, general fatigues & repairs	
Amiens	15th		Battery moved by train to Amiens	
Boves	15th		" " " " Boves	
"	17		25 other ranks at 18th A.R.P.	
"	18		" " " " " 25 other ranks employed on 18th A.R.P Bivouacs prepared ground for	
"	19			
"	20			
"	21			
"	22			
"	23			
"	24			
"	25			
"	26			Returned from 18th A.R.P 21 O.R 15 N.C.O H.Q.
"	27			marched fatigues
"	28			Battery marched by approach to St Ouen area
"	29			
St Ouen	30		Daily parades & fatigues.	

J. Macgregor R.F.A
O.B. x/R T.M.B. 7th Div

WAR DIARY

X/18. Trench Mortar Battery.

MAY 1918.

Place	Date	Hour	Summary of Events and Information	Remarks and references to Appendices
ST OUEN	1/4		Guns of Battery supporting the Lahore Gun Mobile in 15/15 H+S Howitzers	
BEHENCOURT	5		Battery marched with Mtd Divn to BEHENCOURT.	
LINE	6		Made position taken over from the Guns from 11 A.M T.M Battery (Sheet 62 NE) S.H position in W.20.C. (Sheet 57 SE)	
	7		3 Mortars position in E Pad. (Sheet 62 NE) S.H position in W.20.C. (Sheet 57 SE)	
	8/15		3 Mortars positions in W.20.C. (Sheet 57 SE) Rounds used by 4th M.T.M Battery	
	14		One Shrapnel put to support Mtd Inf Bde level positions, but not any ammunition was used	
	15		52 Rounds fired on F.24 b.10.15 and Enemy rifles on E.30.95.10	
	16		2 do 10.10. on B. 14.45 at E.30.95.40 and snipers at E.30.10.15. One shell fell to 20 lbs.	
			After the first round, the rifle and the 15 pounders that seemed to drop very short. Positions shelled & trench destroyed. Night 15/18 spent in holding up snipers & putting Mortars into action	
	16		N.2 Mortar fired 3 rounds on Enemy wires on E.24.95.0 putting the 3 rounds out. Mortar was put out of action by a direct hit from a 10.5 am at 3.45. Sommerville the Batt Officer was seriously wounded.	
	17		Position in E.18 were extended. Mortar ammunition & tackle ammo to went on D.6 a 9.3 Minute got journey to B.11.21 Q x	
	18		Sub tele & ammunition dumped from Lahs to land in D.6.9.3. Mtars on roadway to support Mortars. But kegs & ammunition approach from trail on B.2 M 9.3 by Grenade - B.12.24.8	
	19		Over new positions selected in E.7.d. (Sheet 12 NE)	
	20		Went shelled in new positions in E.7.d. and owing position taken over for observation.	
	21		New positions all under construction	
	22		OP'ble carried out to new position E in Trenches Trench from NE Bn position in E.8.c.40.20 Strong Point	
	23		One new position installed Thursday afts to situation	
	24		B-O Officer in action & enemy fire reported	
	25		Hostile Literature	

Army Form C. 2118.

WAR DIARY
or
INTELLIGENCE SUMMARY

X/12 Trench Mortar Battery

MAY 1918

(Erase heading not required.)

Place	Date	Hour	Summary of Events and Information	Remarks and references to Appendices
LINE	25/28		O.P.s carried out to observe positions & hostile ammunition dumps.	
	29		Postns handed over to X/47 T.M.B. Personnel returned to rest billets in BAIZIEUX	
			Re-positioning HENENCOURT WOOD taken over from X/47, Y/47, Z/47.3 (positions at 24N 90 70) 8×4″ 3 (positions 4.3N 90 60) 5×4″ 3	
BAIZIEUX	30		Battery in rest billets. Usual parties to gun stations.	
	31		Work carried out to complete Bty positions in HENENCOURT WOOD	

J. Allen Capt
re. 12th T.M. Batt.

Army Form C. 2118.

WAR DIARY

X/18. Trench Mortar Battery

INTELLIGENCE SUMMARY

June 1918

Place	Date	Hour	Summary of Events and Information	Remarks and references to Appendices
LINE	1		D.T.M. carried raid on the positions at HENENCOURT WOOD V.26.d.90.70. V.26.d.50.65 (Map Sheet 57D N.E.) The officer reports. Remaining personnel training/parades.	
	2		do	
	3		Daily practice instructing Brigade Lewis Gun Rifle & Gun Staff.	
	4		Reg patrol taken over from Y/18 Trench Mortar Battery V.20.c.0.8, V.20.c.6.2 (Map Sheet 57DNE)	
	5		Patrolling at HENENCOURT WOOD Located new 10"/18.5" Trench Mortar Battery V.26.d.90.70, V.26.d.50.65 (Map Sheet 57DNE)	
	6		Refills at 3 positions V.26.c.3.3, V.26.d.5.2 also shelled 7 A.A. my 12 dwellings to patrol at HENENCOURT WOOD	
	7		Daily training parade.	
	8		Relieved Y/18 Trench Mortar Battery at Patrol Positions (1) M.26.c.3.5 (ii) M.26.c.5.9 (iii) M.26.c.8.4 (iv) M.35.a.0.7 (v) H.31.d.7.9 (vi) M.31.d.20.20 (vii) M.21.a.90.95 (viii) M.21.a.25.65 (ix) M.21.a.10.45 (Map Sheet 57DNE) D.T.M carried out 5 complete patrols & 3 A.A.T.M.	
	9		Saw new position N°9 M.21.a.90.95 & N°10 H.21.a.25.65 complete & ready for mortars. 20 rounds fired on Enemy front line were M.P.s.	
	10		Mortars removed from N°3 positions to D.20.C 16 H.31.a.90.95 & M.21.a.25.65, 135 rounds fired in Enemy front line D.T.M. 7.6.2.D.T.	
	11		187 rounds fired on Enemy front line from N°10 D.T.M. D.T.M. carried on to improve positions	
	12		do do do do Battery relieved by Y/5 Trench Mortar Battery, personnel return to their billets at BAIZIEUX	
BAIZIEUX	13		Daily inspections, Detailed Tactics.	
	14		Battery inspected by Brigadier General W. Evans C.M.G. D.S.O.	
	15		Daily inspection of service.	
	16		Relieved Y/5 Trench Mortar Battery at 5 patrol positions. 28 rounds fired on Enemy front line were D.T.M.	
LINE	17		Own battery T.Msa's. 79 rounds fired on Enemy near R.2.17.A x B r.s.m.	
	18		do do do do do D.T.M	
	19		do do 80 do do do D.T.M	
	20		do do 24 do do do D.T.M. Battery relieved by Y/2 Trench Mortar Battery return to Brigade.	

Army Form C. 2118.

WAR DIARY
or
INTELLIGENCE SUMMARY

X/18 Trench Mortar Battery

June 1918

Place	Date	Hour	Summary of Events and Information	Remarks and references to Appendices
BAIZIEUX	21		Daily inspection of personnel. Gas Respirators at Henencourt Wood completed & mortars maintained ready for action.	
	22		do	
	23		Daily inspection of personnel.	
LIME	24		Relieved 1/5 Trench Mortar Battery at Lavieville Position.	
	25		Line batteries & Personnel proceeded to Law de L'Abbé.	
	26		do	
	27		Orr carried out 15 temporary mortar positions	
	28		160 Rds spent on enemy posts D.21.64b.l.	
BAIZIEUX	29		Battery relieved by 2/18 TMB, personnel billeted in tent lines Baizieux.	
	30		Daily inspection of personnel.	

WAR DIARY

INTELLIGENCE SUMMARY

July 1918

X/18 Trench Mortar Battery.
Ref. Map. Sheet 57D S.E. & AMIENS 1/10,000

461 25

Place	Date	Hour	Summary of Events and Information	Remarks and references to Appendices
BAIZIEUX LINE	1		Inspection & daily practice	
	2		Relieved X/18 at forward positions	
	3		Bud carried up to support trench position & dugouts	
	4		do	
	5		do	
BAIZIEUX	6		Battery relieved by X/18, returned to rest billets	
	7		Inspection & daily practice	
	8		do	
	9		do	
	10		Relieved X/18 at forward positions	
	11		No new fire in enemy trench mortars. Quiet exchange of parties & mg fire	
	12		do	
	13		Bud carried up to position & dugouts	
	14		Battery relieved by X/18 T.M.B. returned to billets at BAIZIEUX & were joined by X/18 C	
BERTRICOURT	15		Inspection & practice of platoons	
	16		Inspection & practice of platoons. Gun drill. Lewis gun & rifle & musketry	
			Musketry. Battery pulled off platoons	
	17		do	
	18		do	
	19		do	
	20		Church parade	
	21		Heavy programme carried out	
	22		do	

Army Form C. 2118.

WAR DIARY
or
INTELLIGENCE SUMMARY.

X/18 Trench Mortar Battery

July 1918

(Erase heading not required.)

Place	Date	Hour	Summary of Events and Information	Remarks and references to Appendices
BERTRICOURT	23		Training Beginners enlisance	
	24		do do do	
	25		do do	
	26		Change of weather	
	27		Tornado enlisance	
	29		do do	
	30		do do	
	31		do do	

18th DIVISION
ARTILLERY

X/18   TRENCH MORTAR BATTERY

AUGUST   1918

Army Form C. 2118.

WAR DIARY
INTELLIGENCE SUMMARY.

(Erase heading not required.)

X 18 Trench Mortar Battery

Place	Date	Hour	Summary of Events and Information	Remarks and references to Appendices
Longpré	Aug 1st		Gun drill, laying & Recuchored draining Ewn carried out	
Lahoussoye	2nd		The battery left Longpré in motor lorries for Lahoussoye	340
"	3rd to 6th		Laying & general fatigues	340
"	7th		The officer & thirty men went forward towards making reconnaissance of trenches North of Sailly-le-Sec. for the artillery to observe after the attack on the morning of 8th	340
"	8th		The above party returned to Lahoussoye	340
"	9th		General fatigues	340
Heilly	10th		Personnel of battery proceeded to Heilly to occupy new billets	340
"	11th to 20th		Gun laying & general fatigues	340
"	21st		Twenty men proceeded to Ammunition Dump for Sheet 62d V.25	
"	22nd to 26th		Personnel of battery employed on Ammunition Dump & doing general fatigues	340

Army Form C. 2118.

WAR DIARY
INTELLIGENCE SUMMARY.
(Erase heading not required.)

X/18 French Mortar Battery

Place	Date	Hour	Summary of Events and Information	Remarks and references to Appendices
HEILLY	27th		Gun laying & fatigues.	
	28th		Personnel moved to E6c3.2 (South End of Albert). Gun stores & supplies etc were up at HEILLY.	
E6c3.2 (Sh 62d NE)	29th to 31		Personnel employed rebuilding Mozeneagos (9.cm) & ammunition dugouts.	
			There were no casualties caused by enemy fire during the month.	

31/4/18

E.E.Mills Lieut R.F.A
O.C. X/18 T.M.B.

Army Form C. 2118.

WAR DIARY
INTELLIGENCE SUMMARY
(Erase heading not required.)

September, 1918.   X.18 Trench M. Mortar Bty   Vol 28

Place	Date	Hour	Summary of Events and Information	Remarks and references to Appendices
Montauban	1st		Personnel engaged on ammunition dumps & general fatigues	
	2nd		One officer & 28 ORs were employed on making and artillery track in True. About 500 yards North of Fregicourt. Rest of personnel on Ammn dumps.	
	3rd		" "	
Combles	4th		The battery less the men on dumps moved to Priez Farm	
"	5th		Personnel employed on Ammunition dumps & general fatigues	
Nurlu	6th		Two 6"TMs were placed in action at D5b21	
Liéramont	7th		The battery less the men on dumps moved to Liéramont	
"	8th		Gun laying, respirator & rifle drill were carried out during the day	
"	9th		" & gun drill, also a general clean up of mortars.	
"	10th to 12th		Personnel employed on ammunition dumps. During this night of the 12th 2 6"TMs were placed in action in front of Peizière (W29b43) & (W29b13).	
"	13th		Registered mortars on the following targets. Wood Farm, Tottenham Post & Railway Triangle at W24d40. Ammn expenditure 24 rnds.	
"	14th		During the night fired 40 rnds on enemy posts in Peizière.	
"	15th		In cooperation with 4" Stokes mortars 50 rounds were fired on to Tottenham & Morgan Posts	
"	16th		Placed 2 more TMs in action in front of Peizière at W29b34. Registered these on Wood Farm. Fired 8 rounds	

Army Form C. 2118.

WAR DIARY
or
INTELLIGENCE SUMMARY.
(Erase heading not required.)

X 18 Trench Mortar Bty

September

Place	Date	Hour	Summary of Events and Information	Remarks and references to Appendices
Lieramont	17th 18th	5.00 p.m.	120 rds were expended during the night on harassing fire at 5.00 p.m. the Infantry attacked the Villages of Peizieres – Epehy. We expended 16 rds. We fired on the following strong points. Tottenham, Morgan & McPhee posts. During the afternoon the Infantry were withdrawn from the line & brought back to Lieramont.	App
"	19th		Two mortars were taken forward & positions occupied in Lempire (F15.b.9.0.)	App
"	20th		Fired 63 rds on X.Y. + Z Copse.	
"	21st		10 rounds were expended on harassing fire.	App
"	22nd		Two positions were reconnoitred at F.16.a.8.6 + mortars placed in action	
"	23rd		Registered Egg Post, Fag Post + Dunham north of West of Fay Support. Amm. expenditure 24 rds. Ref map ♭. 62cNE	
"	24th 25th		Mortars taken out of action & brought back to Lieramont. Personnel engaged cleaning up & refitting.	App
"	From 12th to 25th		10 men were employed on Ammunition dumps. Men withdrawn from dump this evening 25th.	
"	26th		Fatigue pty. + reinforcedr dull were carried out.	App
"	27th		Suddenly NCOs + men left Mr Sarthy Fts. beaucourt to collect a 6" TM town which assembled on the 24th inst. 1 NCO + 4 men to Saulcourt Dump.	App
"	28th		Personnel working on Ammunition dumps. + doing general fatigues	
"	29th		The detachment with mortars proceeded to Lempire.	
"	30th		TM positions were reconnoitred at F.22.d.2.4. but owing to the infantry attack on the Wiseau we withdrew the direction of Vendhuille it was decided to attempt getting the Mortars in action. Mortar dumps withdrawn the afternoon	

WAR DIARY or **INTELLIGENCE SUMMARY**

Army Form C. 2118.

X/18 Trench Mortar Battery
OCTOBER 1918
Ref. Maps: Sheet 62c
57 F S.W. 30

Place	Date	Hour	Summary of Events and Information	Remarks and references to Appendices
LIERAMONT	Oct 1st – 9th		Battery concentrated in camp at LIERAMONT. 13 men on Gen. S.O. A.R.P. BEZIÈRES [Sheet 62c]. Capt. F.C. DUNLOP, O.C. Battery, proceeded on leave 10/10/18 – 24/10/18. Horses & stores to be left at LIERAMONT under charge of...	
LEMPIRE	Oct 13		Battery moved to LEMPIRE [Sheet 62c]	
SERAIN	10th		Battery advanced with 18 Division as far as SERAIN [Sheet 57B]	
BERTRY	Oct 17 – 21st		Moved to BERTRY [57B]. Remaining personnel attached to A.R.P. at BERTRY	
LE CATEAU	Oct 21st 22nd 23rd		Orders received to go into action F.S. of LE CATEAU. Followed reconnaissance, ammunition & motor transport. Party of 20 men relief from Centre as supporting M.L. [Sheet 57B]	
"	Oct 29		Ordered to move to billets in LE CATEAU [Sheet 57B]. Battery moved to farm in 18 Action near ROBERSART. V/15. Relief the gunnery assumed by personnel from R.H. Battery.	
	Oct 29		Capt. E.C. DUNLOP returned from leave as Reserve Commander T.M. Battery having been recommended the full no. nor far men. Total 9 active during 4 Oct 15-23/10/18.	
BOUSIES	Oct 30th		Battery H.Q. moved to BOUSIES [Sheet 57B]. Prisoners taken & F.12c [57B/57B] Registered. 18 surrendered.	
	Oct 31st		Targets given by Infantry Brigade were engaged. £70 rounds expended. The Battery has had 4 Battle Casualties during the month – 1 wounded, 3 wounded (gas). Full operations of the past few days have been rendered exceedingly difficult owing to many of the D.A.C. for all ammunition supply & transport, to make up deficits in G.S. T.M. battery in missing waggons, vehicles & equipments it is essential that transport for ammunition supply etc. should be at the direct & immediate disposal of the battery.	

E.C. Dunlop, Capt. R.F.A.
O.C. X/18 T.M.B.

31/10/18

WAR DIARY

X IV Trench Mortar B'y R.A.

November 1914.

Ref maps: Sheet 57b

Place	Date	Hour	Summary of Events and Information	Remarks and references to Appendices
Bousies	1st to 3rd		Expended 140 rounds on targets in the vicinity of HECQ. [57D NE].	
"	4th		Two mobile mortars manned by personnel of this battery moved forward from Roberscarfaphes. The infantry had gained their first objective, also one mortar detachment was attached to Y Battery for the bombardment, expending 48 rounds.	EQ.
"	5th		The two mobile mortars continued to advance with the infantry but did not come into action. On the morning of the 6th the mortars were marched over to Y Battery, the detachments of the Battery returned to BOUSIES. [Sheet 57b]	N.Q.
"	6th			
Maretz	8th 9th 10th		The Battery marched to Villers at Maretz. Personnel employed cleaning & painting mortars & wagons also on general fatigues.	N.Q.
"	11th		All the personnel engaged sorting ammunition in the vicinity of Busigny Station	N.Q.
"	12th to 30th		1 Officer + 36 O.R. was attached to 53rd Infantry Brigade for the purpose of bailing ammunition in the neighbourhood of Premont. During this month there were no casualties.	N.Q.

E.G. Cavendish Capt.
O/C XIV T.M. B'y R.F.A.
30/11/18

WAR DIARY
or
INTELLIGENCE SUMMARY

December 1918   X/19 Trench Mortar Bty   Army Form C. 2118.

Ref. map [Valenciennes] 57B 30

Place	Date	Hour	Summary of Events and Information	Remarks and references to Appendices
MARETZ	1st to 31st		The officers & 32 O.R. were employed salving ammunition in the neighbourhood of BEAUREVOIR & PREMONT — were attached to the 53rd Infantry Brigade for rations & discipline. 24P	

E.C. Dunlop, Capt
OC X/19th M.B.

1/1/19

JANUARY 1919.

WAR DIARY
INTELLIGENCE SUMMARY.
(Erase heading not required.)

Army Form C. 2118.

X/14 French Mortar

No 16

WM 31

Place	Date	Hour	Summary of Events and Information	Remarks and references to Appendices
"MARETZ"	1st to 31st		One Officer & 30 O.R. were employed salvaging ammunition in the neighbourhood of BEAUREVOIR & were attached to the 53rd Infantry Brigade for rations & discipline etc. Today (31st) this battery was affiliated to the D.A.C. and instructions received from the Divisional Artillery RHQ	

E.C.Dunlop. Capt. R.F.A.
O.C. X/14 T.M.B

31/1/19

Army Form C. 2118

WAR DIARY
or
INTELLIGENCE SUMMARY
(Erase heading not required.)

Instructions regarding War Diaries and Intelligence Summaries are contained in F. S. Regs., Part II. and the Staff Manual respectively. Title Pages will be prepared in manuscript.

Place	Date	Hour	Summary of Events and Information	Remarks and references to Appendices
Rollecourt	1.9.16		Training at Rollecourt	
do.	2.9.16		do. do.	
do.	3.9.16		do. do.	
do.	4.9.16		do. do.	
do.	5.9.16		All medium batteries moved to 5th Army area near Albert (cancelled) remained at Rollecourt.	
do.	6.9.16		Resting at Rollecourt.	
do.	7.9.16		do.	
do.	8.9.16		do.	
Albert	9.9.16		Battery moved into 5th Army area billetting at Albert.	
do.	10.9.16		Resting at Albert.	
do.	11.9.16		do. do.	
do.	12.9.16		Personnel of battery went up to the line to help 83rd Brigade to linew advance gun pits.	
do.	13.9.16		do. do. Still building for 83rd Brigade.	
do.	14.9.16		do. Capt. Bowen expressed a good opinion of the men's work.	

Army Form C. 2118

WAR DIARY
or
INTELLIGENCE SUMMARY
(Erase heading not required.)

Place	Date	Hour	Summary of Events and Information	Remarks and references to Appendices
Albert	15.9.16		Resting at Albert.	
do.	16.9.16		do.	
do.	17.9.16		do. Had Church Parade and H.C. after. R.A.C. Chaplain.	
do.	18.9.16		Battery again helping 82nd Brigade with gun pits. Very wet. Dr. Wilson evacuated to hospital.	
do.	19.9.16		Helping 82nd Brigade. Officers and few men went to Pommelette. Bn. Stang and Lr. Ehrlman wounded by shell fire.	
do.	20.9.16		Helping 82nd Brigade. Finer weather.	
do.	21.9.16		Resting at Albert.	
do.	22.9.16		do. good weather starts again.	
do.	23.9.16		Doing fatigues for R.E.s Brigade at Contalmaison.	
do.	24.9.16		do. do.	
do.	25.9.16		do. do.	
do.	26.9.16		Training at Albert.	
do.	27.9.16		do.	
do.	28.9.16		do.	
do.	29.9.16		do.	
do.	30.9.16		do.	

W.G. Coe Lieut
O.C. V/18. T.M. Bty., R.A.

CONFIDENTIAL

War Diary
of
Y/18 T.M. Battery
f.d.
October 1916

Army Form C. 2118

WAR DIARY
or
INTELLIGENCE SUMMARY
(Erase heading not required.)

Instructions regarding War Diaries and Intelligence Summaries are contained in F.S. Regs., Part II. and the Staff Manual respectively. Title Pages will be prepared in manuscript.

Place	Date	Hour	Summary of Events and Information	Remarks and references to Appendices
In the Field	1-10-16		Battery went up the line to dig positions	
Do	2-10-16		Battery digging positions	
Do	3-10-16		One gun in action. Battery building positions	
Do	4-10-16		Fired eight one gun on point K.23.d.7.6 on enemy sap. 25 rounds fired. 25	
Do	5-10-16		Two guns in action. Opened fire at enemy sap at point K.22.d.75.8. Wire cut in a front of 10 yds and about 8 yds deep. Several more hits were obtained but no gaps were made in wire. One premature burst destroyed one gun pit	
Do	6-10-16		Gaps were cut in enemy's wire at two points. 23.d.7.8. and 23.d.88. both gaps 10 yds wide. Fired also at point K.23.d.72.9. No gaps cut, but hits were obtained around the point somewhere	
Do	7-10-16		Battery building new positions. No firing done. One man at Hosp. (sick)	
Do	8-10-16		Fired at point K.23.d.8.7. Several hits were obtained but no gaps cut. 10 rounds expended. One gun out of action	
Do	9-10-16		Battery building new positions. No firing done. 3 men at Hosp. (sick)	
Do	10-10-16		Battery building new positions. No firing done. Enemy fired a number of Trench Mortars at positions. One falling on a ammunition recess, causing 65 rounds to explode and destroying two gun positions	
Do	11-10-16		Battery building new positions. No firing done	
Do	12-10-16		Fired 33 rounds at point K.23.d.72.9 old gaps made. 3 men at Hosp. 2 wounded by shell fire, one Hell Hosp. Battery relieved at night by 2/18 T.M.B. Effective strength 1 officer and 10 O.R.	
Do	13-10-16		Battery at rest in Cohincamp	
Do	14-10-16		Battery went up the trenches on fatigues for 2/18 T.M. Battery	

N. Goodwin Lieut R.F.A.
O.C. Y/18 T.M. Batty

Army Form C. 2118

WAR DIARY
or
INTELLIGENCE SUMMARY
(Erase heading not required.)

Instructions regarding War Diaries and Intelligence Summaries are contained in F.S. Regs., Part II. and the Staff Manual respectively. Title Pages will be prepared in manuscript.

Place	Date	Hour	Summary of Events and Information	Remarks and references to Appendices
In the Field	15.10.16		Battery went up to the trenches on fatigues for 2/10 T.M.B.	
Do	16.10.16		Battery at rest in Ebincamps	
Do	17.10.16		" " " "	
Do	18.10.16		Reinforcements from D.A.C. 18 Div arrive one officer and 8 O.R. Lieut James J.R. Returned to Base	
Do	19.10.16		Battery went to trenches on fatigues for 2/19 T.M Battery	
Do	20.10.16		Battery relieved 2/18 T.M. Battery	
Do	21.10.16		34 rounds were fired on point 60, plenty of damage was done to wire	
Do	22.10.16		We was out at front W. 46 rounds being fired, one premature burst destroying gun position and wounding Lieut M Good O.C. who was attd to Batty, also Lieut P&J Donnelly was badly shaken 18 rounds were fired at front 60. plenty of damage done to enemys wire. One man atted Mortz(Highr)	
Do	23.10.16		Battery relieved by 2/15 T M Battery	
Do	24.10.16		Battery at rest in Ebincamps. Lieut Donnelly H.J. attd Mortr.	
Do	25.10.16		Battery went up the line on fatigues for 2/15 T.M.B.	
Do	26.10.16		do do do	
Do	27.10.16		do do do	
Do	28.10.16		Battery went up to the trenches to take to charge from out of action	
Do	29.10.16		Battery at rest in Ebincamps	
Do	30.10.16		Battery in Training at Ebincamps do do	
Do	31.10.16		do " do do	

War Diary
for
November 1916

Y/18 M.T.M. B'ty

Army Form C. 2118

WAR DIARY
or
INTELLIGENCE SUMMARY
(Erase heading not required.)

Instructions regarding War Diaries and Intelligence Summaries are contained in F. S. Regs., Part II. and the Staff Manual respectively. Title Pages will be prepared in manuscript.

Place	Date	Hour	Summary of Events and Information	Remarks and references to Appendices
In the Field	1-11-16		Battery at rest in Bollincamps	
	2-11-16		" " " "	
	3-11-16		" " " "	
	4-11-16		" " " "	
	5-11-16		" " " "	
	6-11-16		Lieut W Good O.C. returned to unit from R.G.A. Base Depot.	
	7-11-16		" " " "	
	8-11-16		" " " "	
	9-11-16		" " " "	
	10-11-16		" " " "	
	11-11-16		Battery on Fatigue for D.T.M.O. 31st Division	
	12-11-16		" " " "	
	13-11-16		Battery at rest	
	14-11-16		" " " "	
	15-11-16		" " " "	
	16-11-16		Battery moved by Lorry from Bollincamps to Albert to form 18th Division arrived in Albert this same day.	
	17-11-16		Battery on Fatigue for R.E. 18th Div at MENLUY (Woodcutting)	
	18-11-16			
	19-11-16			
	20-11-16			
	21-11-16			

Army Form C. 2118

WAR DIARY
or
INTELLIGENCE SUMMARY

(Erase heading not required.)

Instructions regarding War Diaries and Intelligence Summaries are contained in F. S. Regs., Part II. and the Staff Manual respectively. Title Pages will be prepared in manuscript.

Place	Date	Hour	Summary of Events and Information	Remarks and references to Appendices
In the Field	22.11.16		Battery on Fatigues for R.E. 18th Div. at MELUY (WOODCUTTING)	
	23.11.16		Battery at rest. Bathing Parade.	
	24.11.16		Battery on Fatigues for R.E. 18th Div. at AVELUY (WOODCUTTING)	
	25.11.16		" " " " " " " "	
	26.11.16		" " " " " " " "	
	27.11.16		Parades for Inspection of Battery Arms, equipment	
	28.11.16		" " " " Rifles, smoke helmets and respirators	
	29.11.16		Battery on Fatigues for TOWN MAJOR. Inspection of Battery	
	30.11.16		" " " " " " " "	

W. Good Lieut.
O.C./18 T.M. Bty.

Confidential
War Diary of
"Y" 1st Trench Mortar Battery

From December 1st 1916 to December 31st 1916.

(Volume VI)

Army Form C. 2118

WAR DIARY
or
INTELLIGENCE SUMMARY
(Erase heading not required.)

Instructions regarding War Diaries and Intelligence Summaries are contained in F.S. Regs., Part II. and the Staff Manual respectively. Title Pages will be prepared in manuscript.

Place	Date	Hour	Summary of Events and Information	Remarks and references to Appendices
In the Field	1/12/16		Battery stood by for fatigues for Town Major ALBERT	
"	2/12/16		Battery prepared to move to new area. Orders fail to come.	
"	3/12/16		Battery move to PETIT PORT by lorry from ALBERT arrive the same day	
"	4/12/16		General Fatigues and Parades Inspection of Rifles ect	
"	5/12/16		Battery at rest. Fatigues and Inspection	
"	6/12/16		"	
"	7/12/16		"	
"	8/12/16		"	
"	9/12/16		"	Rifles Inspect
"	10/12/16		"	
"	11/12/16		"	Revolver Practice
"	12/12/16		"	
"	13/12/16		"	
"	14/12/16		Battery on fatigues for 82nd Col BELERA	Bathing Parade
"	15/12/16		"	"
"	16/12/16		"	Bathing Parade

1875 Wt. W593/826 1,000,000 4/15 I.B.C. & A. A.D.S.S./Forms/C. 2118.

WAR DIARY
or
INTELLIGENCE SUMMARY

(Erase heading not required.)

Army Form C. 2118

Instructions regarding War Diaries and Intelligence Summaries are contained in F. S. Regs., Part II. and the Staff Manual respectively. Title Pages will be prepared in manuscript.

Place	Date	Hour	Summary of Events and Information	Remarks and references to Appendices
In the Field	17.12.16		CHURCH PARADE	
"	18.12.16		Fatigues for 82nd Bde. R.F.A. 18 Div	
"	19.12.16		" " " " "	
"	20.12.16		" " " " "	
"	21.12.16		" " " " "	
"	22.12.16		" " " " "	
"	23.12.16		" " " " "	
"	24.12.16		" " " " "	
"	25.12.16		Battery fatigues CHURCH PARADE	
"	26.12.16		" " "	
"	27.12.16		" " "	
"	28.12.16		Battery left PETITPORT to join 61st D.A.C. Moved to ABBEVILLE for the night.	
"	29.12.16		Battery moved by train from ABBEVILLE to ACHVEX arrived the second day. Third G.S. Waggon from 61st D.A.C. awaiting. Three were loaded and Dispatched. Personnel of Battery and remainder of Horses stayed at ACHVEX for the night.	
"	30.12.16		Batteries Personnel and Horses moved to 61st D.A.C.	
"	31.12.16		Battery Fatigues, also 5 men for fatigues at 61st D.A.C. Hqrs	

Army Form C. 2118

WAR DIARY
or
INTELLIGENCE SUMMARY
(Erase heading not required.)

Instructions regarding War Diaries and Intelligence Summaries are contained in F.S. Regs., Part II. and the Staff Manual respectively. Title Pages will be prepared in manuscript.

Place	Date	Hour	Summary of Events and Information	Remarks and references to Appendices
In the Field	1-1-17		All available men on Fatigues for Division Headqrs	
"	2-1-17		Do	
"	3-1-17		Do	
"	4-1-17		Do	
"	5-1-17		Do	
"	6-1-17		Do	
"	7-1-17		Do	
"	8-1-17		Do	
"	9-1-17		Do	
"	10-1-17		Do	
"	11-1-17		Do	
"	12-1-17		Battery moved from 18th Divl R.A. area to BLIGHTY WOOD	
"	13-1-17		All available men on Fatigues for 82nd Bde R.F.A.	
"	14-1-17		Do	
"	15-1-17		Fatigue Party of 7 for 84th Bde and a Fatigue Party of 7 for 82nd Bde	
"	16-1-17		Do	
"	17-1-17		Do	
"	18-1-17		Do	
"	19-1-17		Do	
"	20-1-17		Do	

N. G. ODD Lieut.
O.C. Y/18 T.M. Bty
R.A.

Army Form C. 2118

WAR DIARY
or
INTELLIGENCE SUMMARY
(*Erase heading not required.*)

Place	Date	Hour	Summary of Events and Information	Remarks and references to Appendices
In the Field	21-1-17		All available men on Fatigues for 82nd Bde R.F.A.	
Do	22-1-17		Do	
Do	23-1-17		Do	
Do	24-1-17		Do	
Do	25-1-17		Do	
Do	26-1-17		Do	
Do	27-1-17		Do	
Do	28-1-17		Do	
Do	29-1-17		Do	
Do	30-1-17		Do	
Do	31-1-17		Do	

W. Good Lieut.
O.C. Y/15. T.M. Bty.
R.A.

Army Form C. 2118

WAR DIARY
or
INTELLIGENCE SUMMARY
(Erase heading not required.)

Instructions regarding War Diaries and Intelligence Summaries are contained in F. S. Regs., Part II. and the Staff Manual respectively. Title Pages will be prepared in manuscript.

Place	Date	Hour	Summary of Events and Information	Remarks and references to Appendices
In the Field	1-2-17		All available men on Fatigues for 82nd Bde RFA	
Do	2-2-17		Do	
Do	3-2-17		Do	
Do	4-2-17		Do	
Do	5-2-17		Do	
Do	6-2-17		Do	
Do	7-2-17		Do	
Do	8-2-17		Do	
Do	9-2-17		Do	
Do	10-2-17		Three men on Fatigues for 83rd Bde remainder on Fatigues for 82nd Bde RFA	
Do	11-2-17		Do	
Do	12-2-17		Do	
Do	13-2-17		Do	
Do	14-2-17		Do	
Do	15-2-17		All available men on Fatigues unloading ammunition at NAB SIDING and taking the same to AVD Stations of the 83rd Bde	
Do	16-2-17		All available men unloading ammunition and loading the same for Batteries of the 10th Division	
Do	17-2-17		20 men on Fatigues for 84th Bde RFA	
Do	18-2-17		Do	
Do	19-2-17		Do	

W. Good Lieut.
O.E. Y/15 T. M. B. Ty. R.A.

Army Form C. 2118

WAR DIARY
or
INTELLIGENCE SUMMARY

(Erase heading not required.)

Instructions regarding War Diaries and Intelligence Summaries are contained in F. S. Regs., Part II. and the Staff Manual respectively. Title Pages will be prepared in manuscript.

Place	Date	Hour	Summary of Events and Information	Remarks and references to Appendices
In the Field	20.2.17		All available N.C.Os and men of fatigues for 82nd Bde. R.F.A.	
Do	21.2.17		Do	
Do	22.2.17		Do	
Do	23.2.17		Do	
Do	24.2.17		Do	
Do	25.2.17		Battery Recruits by for Orders	
Do	26.2.17		All available N.C.Os and men on fatigues for D.A.C. & Div removing ammunition & dump	
Do	27.2.17		Do	
Do	28.2.17		Do	

W. Good Lieut
O.C. Y/18 T.M. Bty, R.A.

War Diary
for
March. 1917

X. Y. & Z/18
Trench Mortar
Batteries

Army Form C. 2118

WAR DIARY
or
INTELLIGENCE SUMMARY
(Erase heading not required.)

Instructions regarding War Diaries and Intelligence Summaries are contained in F.S. Regs, Part II. and the Staff Manual respectively. Title Pages will be prepared in manuscript.

Place	Date	Hour	Summary of Events and Information	Remarks and references to Appendices
In the Field	1.3.17		12 N.C.O's and men on Fatigues for D.A.C. 18th Div from 8.00 am till 4.0 pm. Paraded again at 9.30 pm till 6.0 am on the 2nd	
Do	2.3.17		Remainder of day at rest	
Do	3.3.17		7 men on Fatigues for D.A.C. 18th Div	
Do	4.3.17		Fatigues for D.A.C. 18th Div	
Do	5.3.17		Do	
Do	6.3.17		Do	
Do	7.3.17		Do	
Do	8.3.17		Battery moved by Lorry from AUTHUILLE WOOD to ARRAS. Arrived at ABUIGNY EN ARTOIS the same day. Stayed at the afore mentioned place for the night	
Do	9.3.17		Stayed at ABUIGNY EN ARTOIS. Rifle and Pistol inspection.	
Do	10.3.17		Left ABUIGNY EN ARTOIS to join 9th Div at ARRAS arrived at ARRAS the same day and billeted in 9th Div area.	
Do	11.3.17		Went to trenches with 9 D.T.M.O. and took over 6 Battle Emplacements	
Do	12.3.17		Two Guns were taken up at night	
Do	13.3.17		Two Guns in Action	
Do	14.3.17		Registered on point J.12.c.58.0. N° of rounds fired 31. Two Gaps were made. Enemy retaliated with ng.14 Field Guns. No firing was carried out during the day owing to no ammunition being received. Work was carried out improving positions.	

W. Good Lieut.

Army Form C. 2118

WAR DIARY
or
INTELLIGENCE SUMMARY

(Erase heading not required.)

Place	Date	Hour	Summary of Events and Information	Remarks and references to Appendices
In the Field	16.3.17		Fired at enemy wire at point g.12.d.5.76 a gap of about 20 yds wide was cut at this point also at points g.12.c.5.5 and g.12.c.6.8, a gap about 8 yds wide was cut. 40 of rounds fired 42. two of which failed to explode. Retaliation from enemy was slight.	
Do	18.3.17		Gaps reported yesterday between points g.12.c.5.8 and g.12.c.6.8 have all been made wider. The average width being about 15 yds, one new gap was made at point g.12.c.6.58 this was about one yds wide. Heavy retaliation was made by the enemy. Number of rounds fired 30.	
Do	17.3.17		During the night the enemy damaged one of our emplacements by shell fire putting the gun out of action pro tem. 28 rounds were fired between points g.12.s.8.5 and g.12.c.5.c.8 the wire was very badly damaged. The enemy retaliated very heavily. Two more guns were taken up at night.	
Do	18.3.17		The two guns taken up last night put in action. Registered on points g.12.c.6.49 and g.12.a.7.2 round fells were obtained on these points. Number of rounds fired 32. Enemy did not retaliate.	
Do	19.3.17		70 rounds were fired at our at points g.12.a.6.23 one small gap was made also another small gap was made at point g.12.c.69. Several hits were obtained at other places and much damage done, but of the 70 rounds fired 18 failed to explode. In my opinion this was due to the strong winds blowing at the time of firing. The enemy retaliated much by light field guns	
Do	20.3.17		50 rounds were fired at enemy wire at point g.12.c.6.9 r g.12.a.4.2 several hits were made also between points g.12.c.6.9 & g.12.a.4.2 several hits were obtained. Slight retaliation was made by the enemy.	

W. Good Lieut.

Army Form C. 2118

WAR DIARY
or
INTELLIGENCE SUMMARY
(Erase heading not required.)

Instructions regarding War Diaries and Intelligence Summaries are contained in F. S. Regs., Part II. and the Staff Manual respectively. Title Pages will be prepared in manuscript.

Place	Date	Hour	Summary of Events and Information	Remarks and references to Appendices
In the Field	21.3.17		No ammunition was fired at enemy seen to-day, owing to a big raid being carried out by our Infantry. 72 rounds were fired at enemy trenches on the night flank of our advancing party during this operation with good results. The Stokesmin of the enemy were very noisy indeed.	
Do	22.3.17		Several small gaps were made in enemy wire between points g.12.c.6.9. and g.12.a.7.3. 48 rounds were fired of which 8 failed to explode. Slight retaliation by enemy on July communication trench with Field Guns.	
Do	23.3.17		68 rounds were fired on enemys wire between points g.12.c.5.3. and g.12.c.5.7. 3 large gaps were made in enemy wire. The enemy did not retaliate.	
Do	24.3.17		4 small gaps were made in wire between points g.12.c.6.9 and g.12.a.7.3. 80 rounds were fired between the latter points. The enemys retaliation was very heavy and did not on one of our emplacements but the gun was out of action.	
Do	25.3.17		60 rounds were fired on wire between points g.12.c.3.8 and g.12.a.3.2. 2 small gaps were made. The enemy slightly retaliated with field guns.	
Do	26.3.17		One gap was cut in enemy wire at point g.12.a.7.3. 48 rounds were fired & little delay was caused by rifle mechanism, which threw out of gun. The enemy did not retaliate. Observation was very bad.	
Do	27.3.17		Wire was cut between points g.12.c.6.9 and g.12.a.5.3. The 21st round was a premature burst which destroyed the gun emplacement & also killed one O.R. and WOUNDED one O.R.	

W. Goodredt

Army Form C. 2118.

WAR DIARY
or
INTELLIGENCE SUMMARY

(Erase heading not required.)

Instructions regarding War Diaries and Intelligence Summaries are contained in F. S. Regs., Part II. and the Staff Manual respectively. Title Pages will be prepared in manuscript.

Place	Date	Hour	Summary of Events and Information	Remarks and references to Appendices
In the Field	28.3.17		No ammunition was fired owing to 6 guns being out of action. Work was carried on in gun emplacements who storing ammunition.	
Do	29.3.17		Work on positions was carried on and storing ammunition.	
Do	30.3.17		Do	
Do	31.3.17		Do	

W. Good Lieut
O.C. X/18 T.M. Bty.

Army Form C. 2118.

WAR DIARY
or
INTELLIGENCE SUMMARY
(Erase heading not required.)

Place	Date	Hour	Summary of Events and Information	Remarks and references to Appendices
In the Field	1-4-17		Work was carried on building gun positions and storing ammunition	
Do	2.4.17		Do	
Do	3.4.17		Do	3 gun in action
Do	4.4.17		Two hundred and nineteen rounds were fired on enemy wire, 2 gaps made between points y.12.a.6.3. and y.12.a.6.3.4, being obliterated with by by field guns. One shed broke after firing 20 rounds also a record had been made of hits scoring into gun pit. To be relayed serving 16 which flouting into gun pit.	
Do	5.4.17		250 rounds fired on enemy wire and front line trench, one gap was cut at front y.12.a.7.2.3, also several hits were obtained on front line trench between Sap V.13 and Sap V.14. A lot of trouble was caused by rifle mechanism, from became useless.	
Do	6.4.17		Gap was cut in enemy wire at point y.12.a.65.40 and several hits were obtained on enemy front line between Sap V.15 and Sap V.13 256 rounds were fired. Enemy retaliated with trench mortar and field battery. The same trouble was experienced to if item being unfit for further use, such Rifle mechanism.	
Do	7.4.17		All firing was on enemy trenches between Sap V.15 and Sap V.13, 202 rounds were fired, slight retaliation by enemy. Trench Dugouts much inconvenient. 8 were unfit for further use.	W. Goodhead O.C. 1/16 Th M.B. H

Army Form C. 2118.

WAR DIARY
or
INTELLIGENCE SUMMARY
(Erase heading not required.)

Instructions regarding War Diaries and Intelligence Summaries are contained in F. S. Regs., Part II. and the Staff Manual respectively. Title Pages will be prepared in manuscript.

Place	Date	Hour	Summary of Events and Information	Remarks and references to Appendices
In the Field	8.4.17		156 rounds were fired on enemy front and support line between Sap V.15 top V.13. Several direct hits were obtained. Enemy retaliation by enemy.	
Do	9.4.17		All ammunition was rendered unfit for further use.	
"	10.4.17		Battery marching by for orders. One O.R. wounded.	
"	11.4.17		All guns and section out of action and brought down to billets in ARRAS.	
"	12.4.17		Battery fatigues. All guns, stores and Rifles inspected.	
"	13.4.17		Battery fatigues and inspections.	
"	14.4.17		Battery fatigues and inspections. 5 O.R. on fatigues for 9th D.T.M.B.	
"	15.4.17		Battery fatigues and inspections	
"	16.4.17		Do	
"	17.4.17		Do	
"	18.4.17		Do	
"	19.4.17		Do	

W. Good Lieut.
O.C. Y/15 T.M.B. 4p.

Army Form C. 2118.

WAR DIARY
or
INTELLIGENCE SUMMARY

(Erase heading not required.)

Instructions regarding War Diaries and Intelligence Summaries are contained in F.S. Regs., Part II. and the Staff Manual respectively. Title Pages will be prepared in manuscript.

Place	Date	Hour	Summary of Events and Information	Remarks and references to Appendices
In the Field	20.4.17		Battery fatigues and Kit prelims	
Do	21.4.17		Do	
Do	22.4.17		Do	
Do	23.4.17		Do	
Do	24.4.17		Do	
Do	25.4.17		Do	
Do	26.4.17		Do	
Do	27.4.17		Do	
Do	28.4.17		Battery moved by lorries from 9th Div ARRAS to join 18th Div arrived at PERNES same day. Stopped for the night	
Do	29.4.17		moved from PERNES to 18th Div area BEAURAINS arrived same day	
Do	30.4.17		Battery fatigues	

W. Good Lieut.
O.C. Y/18 T.M.B.

Army Form C. 2118

WAR DIARY
or
INTELLIGENCE SUMMARY
(Erase heading not required.)

Instructions regarding War Diaries and Intelligence Summaries are contained in F. S. Regs., Part II. and the Staff Manual respectively. Title Pages will be prepared in manuscript.

Place	Date	Hour	Summary of Events and Information	Remarks and references to Appendices
In the Field	1-5-17		Butting fatigues, Inspection and Drills	
Do	2-5-17		Do	
Do	3-5-17		Do	
Do	4-5-17		Do	
Do	5-5-17		Do	
Do	6-5-17		Do	
Do	7-5-17		Do	
Do	8-5-17		Do	
Do	9-5-17		Do	also guns and Personnel inspected by G.O.C.R.A. 18th Div
Do	10-5-17		Do	
Do	11-5-17		Do	
Do	12-5-17		Do	
Do	13-5-17		Do	
Do	14-5-17		Do	
Do	15-5-17		Do	
Do	16-5-17		Do	
Do	17-5-17		Do	
Do	18-5-17		All available N.C.O.s and men on fatigue for D/83 (Temporarily attd.)	
Do	19-5-17		Do	

N. Wood Lieut.
O.C. Y/18 T.M.B Hy

Army Form C. 2118

WAR DIARY
or
INTELLIGENCE SUMMARY
(Erase heading not required.)

Instructions regarding War Diaries and Intelligence Summaries are contained in F. S. Regs., Part II. and the Staff Manual respectively. Title Pages will be prepared in manuscript.

Place	Date	Hour	Summary of Events and Information	Remarks and references to Appendices
In the Field	20.5.17		All available N.C.O.'s and Men on Fatigues for D/83 Bde RFA. Transpt attd	
Do	21.5.17		Do	
Do	22.5.17		Do	
Do	23.5.17		Do	1 gun and Ammn handed over to
Do	24.5.17		Do	V/33.T.M.B. 4 guns transferred when
Do	25.5.17		Do	over and 3rd Army School of
Do	26.5.17		Do	Mortars
Do	27.5.17		Do	
Do	28.5.17		Do	
Do	29.5.17		Do	
Do	30.5.17		Do	
Do	31.5.17		Do	

W. Good Lieut.
O.C. V/18. T.M.Bty

Army Form C. 2118

WAR DIARY
or
INTELLIGENCE SUMMARY
(Erase heading not required.)

Instructions regarding War Diaries and Intelligence Summaries are contained in F.S. Regs., Part II. and the Staff Manual respectively. Title Pages will be prepared in manuscript.

Place	Date	Hour	Summary of Events and Information	Remarks and references to Appendices
In the Field	1-6-17		Battery on Fatigues for D/83 Bde R.F.A.	
Do	2-6-17		Remainder of Battery and Battery Stores move by L.S. Waggons from BEAURAINS to HENIN. All available NCO's and Men on fatigues for D/83 Bde R.F.A.	
Do	3-6-17		All available NCO's and men on Fatigues for B/83" Bde R.F.A.	
Do	4-6-17		Do	
Do	5-6-17		Do	
Do	6-6-17		Do	
Do	7-6-17		Do	
Do	8-6-17		Do	
Do	9-6-17		Do	
Do	10-6-17		Do	
Do	11-6-17		Do	
Do	12-6-17		Do	
Do	13-6-17		Do	
Do	14-6-17		All NCOs and Men returned to unit for Redistribution & reissue of Battery personnel, equipment and clothes.	
Do	15-6-17		8 NCO's and Men to B/83 Bde and 4 NCO's and Men to C/83 for Fatigues	
Do	16-6-17		Do	
Do	17-6-17		Do	
Do	18-6-17		All available NCOs and men on Fatigues for B/83 Bde R.F.A.	
Do	19-6-17		Do	

Army Form C. 2118

WAR DIARY
or
INTELLIGENCE SUMMARY

(Erase heading not required.)

Instructions regarding War Diaries and Intelligence Summaries are contained in F. S. Regs., Part II. and the Staff Manual respectively. Title Pages will be prepared in manuscript.

Place	Date	Hour	Summary of Events and Information	Remarks and references to Appendices
In the Field	20.6.17		All available NCOs and men on Fatigues	
Do	21.6.17		All NCOs and men return to Unit	
Do	22.6.17		Battery Fatigues. Parades for Inspection	
Do	23.6.17		Do Foot Drill, Rifle Drill et	
Do	24.6.17		Do Do Gun Respirator Drill	
Do	25.6.17		Do Do	
Do	26.6.17		Do Do	
Do	27.6.17		Battery moved by G.S. Wagons from HENIN to Dunnencourt Rd Camp	
Do	28.6.17		6 men on Fatigues for Divisional Athletic Sports, Remainder Battery Fatigues	
Do	29.6.17		8 men on Fatigues for Divisional Athletic Sports Do	
Do	30.6.17		Do Do Do	

W. Good Lieut. R.G.A.
O.C. Y/15 T.M.B.

Army Form C. 2118

WAR DIARY
or
INTELLIGENCE SUMMARY
(Erase heading not required.)

Instructions regarding War Diaries and Intelligence Summaries are contained in F. S. Regs, Part II. and the Staff Manual respectively. Title Pages will be prepared in manuscript.

Place	Date	Hour	Summary of Events and Information	Remarks and references to Appendices
In the Field	1-7-17		6 men on Fatigues for Divisional sports. Remainder Fatigues and Drills.	
Do	2-7-17		Battery Fatigues. Remainder of the day for attending Sports.	
Do	3-7-17		Battery moved by lorry from Div Rest Area to DOULLENS arrived the same day	
Do	4-7-17		Battery entrain at DOULLENS and detrained at GODAERVELDT at 12.30am arrived the same day	
Do	5-7-17		Battery marched to Billets outside STEENVOORDE. All Horses and Kit brought by lorry from Wailer	
Do	6-7-17		Battery Fatigues, Inspections, S.B.R. Drills and Gun Cleaning.	
Do	7-7-17		Do marching drill and gun drill.	
Do	8-7-17		Do Inspections gun drill and Fatigues	
Do	9-7-17		Battery Fatigues, Gun drill and Cleaning	
Do	10-7-17		Battery Fatigues Inspection, S.B.R. Drill.	
Do	11-7-17		Battery Fatigues Gun Cleaning, Gun drill and marching drill.	
Do	12-7-17		Battery moved by lorry from STEENVOORDE and arrived at billets outside DICKYBUSCH arrived 3 min to 30 P.M.	
Do	13-7-17		1 NCO and 3 men to 30th A.R.P for fatigues also 4 men for D/83 Bde	
Do	14-7-17		Do	
Do	15-7-17		Do	N. G. Goodwent M.B. O.L. 7/Lieut T.M.B.

WAR DIARY
or
INTELLIGENCE SUMMARY

(Erase heading not required.)

Army Form C.-2118

Instructions regarding War Diaries and Intelligence Summaries are contained in F. S. Regs., Part II. and the Staff Manual respectively. Title Pages will be prepared in manuscript.

Place	Date	Hour	Summary of Events and Information	Remarks and references to Appendices
In the Field	16.7.17		1 N.C.O. and 4 men on Z JO & A.R.P. for Fatigues	
Do	17.7.17		Battery Fatigues, Repairing drills etc	
Do	18.7.17		Do	
Do	19.7.17		Do	
Do	20.7.17		Do	
Do	21.7.17		Do	
Do	22.7.17		4 O.R on Fatigues for the new A.R.P.	
Do	23.7.17		Battery Repairing, S.B.A Drill etc	
Do	24.7.17		Do	
Do	25.7.17		All available N.C.O's and men for fatigues carrying Bombs for 2/1.5 Trench mortar Battery	
Do	26.7.17		Battery Fatigues, Repairing etc	
Do	27.7.17		4 men on Fatigues for A 52nd Bde also 4 for Fatigues for B/82 Bde	
Do	28.7.17		Do	
Do	29.7.17		One N.C.O and 6 Men on Fatigues at the new A.R.P.	
Do	30.7.17		1 O.R on Fatigues for B/83	
Do	31.7.17		All available N.C.Os and men to report for trenches tomorrow	W.G.god Lieut O.C. 1/15 T.M. B.y

WAR DIARY
or
INTELLIGENCE SUMMARY

Army Form C. 2118

Place	Date	Hour	Summary of Events and Information	Remarks and references to Appendices
In the Field	1-8-17		One N.C.O. and 4 men temporarily attached to "B" Battery, 82nd Bde. RFA, 18th Division. Two N.C.O. and 7 men temporarily attached to "D" Battery, 82nd Bde RFA, 18th Div. on Fatigue gun cleaning &c.	
Do	2-8-17		Do	
	3-8-17		Do	
	4-8-17		Do	
	5-8-17		Do	
	6-8-17		Do	
	7-8-17		Do	
	8-8-17		Do	
	9-8-17		Do	
	10-8-17		Do	
	11-8-17		Do	
	12-8-17		Do	
	13-8-17		Do	
	14-8-17		Do	
	15-8-17		Do	
	16-8-17		Do	
	17-8-17		Do	
	18-8-17		Do	
	19-8-17		Do	

Army Form C. 2118.

WAR DIARY
or
INTELLIGENCE SUMMARY.
(Erase heading not required)

Place	Date	Hour	Summary of Events and Information	Remarks and references to Appendices
In Field	20.8.17		5 OR temporarily attached to B Battery 82nd Bde. R.F.A. 18th Division, 9 OR Temporarily attached to D Battery 82nd Bde R.F.A. 18th Division. Remain on Battery Fatigues, Gun cleaning act	
Do	21.8.17		Do	
Do	22.8.17		Do	
Do	23.8.17		Do	
Do	24.8.17		Do	
Do	25.8.17		Do	
Do	26.8.17		Do	
Do	27.8.17		Do	
Do	28.8.17		All OR's return to Battery for one day for the purpose of Coy Commanders Inspection on the 28.8.17 Coy Commanders Inspection cancelled all OR's return to respective Batteries	
Do	29.8.17		5 O.R. at B/82nd Bde R.F.A. 9 OR at D/82nd Bde R.F.A. remain on Battery Fatigues act	
Do	30.8.17		Battery moved from (Forward Area Trench Weapons Camp Butty) to back Area OUDEZEELE by tram lorry arrived the same day	PICKEBUSCH
Do	31.8.17		Battery Inspection Drills act	J. Carter 2/Lt R.F.A. for O/c Y/18 T.M.B. R.A.

Army Form C. 2118.

WAR DIARY
INTELLIGENCE SUMMARY.
(Erase heading not required.)

Y/18 Dn Batt

Instructions regarding War Diaries and Intelligence Summaries are contained in F.S. Regs., Part II. and the Staff Manual respectively. Title pages will be prepared in manuscript.

Place	Date	Hour	Summary of Events and Information	Remarks and references to Appendices
In the Field	1-9-17		Battery Fatigues, Inspection and Gun Drill	
	2-9-17		Battery Fatigues Inspection, Gun Cleaning and Gun Drill	
	3-9-17		Battery Practice with Demonrad Artillery for Inspection by J.O.C. RA.18 Div. also Inspection of awards by G.O.C. II Corps	
	4-9-17		Battery Fatigues, Inspection, Gun Cleaning and Rifle Practice	
	5-9-17		Battery Fatigues, Inspection of Rifle and Pistol Inspection and Drill with Gas appliances	
	6-9-17		Battery Fatigues and Inspections, Gun Cleaning and Drill Musical Practice	
	7-9-17		Battery Fatigues and Inspection, Box Respirator Drill	
	8-9-17		Battery Fatigues and Inspection Drill with P.H. and Box Respirators	
	9-9-17		All Ranks paraded for scratch trip	
	10-9-17		Battery Fatigues Inspections Gun Cleaning Box Respirator Drill	
	11-9-17		Battery Fatigues Inspection, Gun Drill, Rifle Inspection and Drill	
	12-9-17		Battery Fatigues Inspection, Rifle Practice and Rifle Inspection	
	13-9-17		Battery Fatigues Inspection, Gun Cleaning, Gun Drill and Rifle Drill	
	14-9-17		Battery Fatigues Inspection Marching Drill and Gun Cleaning	
	15-9-17		Battery Fatigues Inspection, Box Respirator Inspection and Drill	
	16-9-17		Battery Fatigues Inspection Musketry Practice, and Box Respirator Drill	

WAR DIARY

INTELLIGENCE SUMMARY.

(Erase heading not required.)

Army Form C. 2118.

Instructions regarding War Diaries and Intelligence Summaries are contained in F. S. Regs., Part II. and the Staff Manual respectively. Title pages will be prepared in manuscript.

Place	Date	Hour	Summary of Events and Information	Remarks and references to Appendices
In the Field	17-7-17		Battery Fatigues, Inspection, Rifle Inspection, Gun Drill and Cleaning	
"	18-7-17		Battery Fatigues, Inspection. Box Respirator and P.H. Helmet Drill	
"	19-7-17		Battery Fatigues, Inspection, Rifle Inspection and musketry	
"	20-7-17		Battery moved by lorry from OUDEZEELE to SERQUES arrived the same day	
"	21-7-17		Battery Fatigues, Inspection. Improvement of Camp, gun cleaning and Inspection of Arms.	
"	22-7-17		Battery Fatigues - Inspection. Gun cleaning and Drill with Gas appliances	
"	23-7-17		Battery Fatigues, Inspections, Marching Drill and Rifle Drill	
"	24-7-17		11 O.R. sent to D.A.C. 18th Div. Remainder moved by lorry from SERQUES to ZEGGERS CAPPEL arrived the same day	
"	25-7-17		Battery moved by lorry from ZEGGERS CAPPEL to POPERINGHE arrived the same day	
"	26-7-17		Battery Fatigues, Inspection, cleaning guns and Hiring for Inspection	
"	27-7-17		Battery Fatigues, Inspections and Rifle Drill	
"	28-7-17		Battery Fatigues, Inspection of P.H. Helmets. Battery moved by G.S. Wagons from POPERINGHE to VLAMERTINGHE and took over Pulled Teams the 48th Divisional Trench Mortars.	

Army Form C. 2118.

WAR DIARY
or
INTELLIGENCE SUMMARY
(Erase heading not required.)

Place	Date	Hour	Summary of Events and Information	Remarks and references to Appendices
In the Field	29.9.17		Battling Fatigues Cleaning Camps and Movement of Billets cleaning Guns and Equipment.	
	30.9.17		One Officer and 9 O.R. proceeded at 10 am to proceed to 291 Bde R.F.A. for fatigue work. One Officer at A.R.P. and one O.R.	

Refll.H.Y.
4/8 T.M.B.

Army Form C. 2118.

WAR DIARY
or
INTELLIGENCE SUMMARY.
(Erase heading not required.)

1/18 Trench Mortar Battery

Place	Date	Hour	Summary of Events and Information	Remarks and references to Appendices
In the Field	1/10/17		1 Officer and 10 O.R. att 291 Bde R.F.A. for Fatigues, remainder Camp Fatigues, Battery Fatigues, Inspections.	
"	2/10/17		2 O.R. to C/83 Bde. for Fatigues, remainder the same day, remainder Gun cleaning	
"	3/10/17		5 O.R. returned from 291 Bde R.F.A. Battery Fatigues and Gun Cleaning	
"	4/10/17		3 O.R. to C/83 Bde RFA for one days fatigues, remainder general Fatigues	
"	5/10/17		2 O.R. to C/53 Bde RFA for one days fatigues, remainder Gun cleaning	
"	6/10/17		Battery Fatigues and Inspections	
"	7/10/17		1 Officer and 5 O.R. returned from 291 Bde R.F.A. remainder fatigues	
"	8/10/17		Battery fatigues, Inspection, Gun Cleaning, and Rifle Inspection	
"	9/10/17		Do	
"	10/10/17		C.O.R. to A.R.P. for Fatigues	
"	11/10/17		Moved by G.S. Wagons from (Rugbert Huts) VLAMERTINGHE to TRES TROYS and both over Billets from the 11th Divn T.M.R.	
"	12/10/17		Cleaning Billets, Improvement of Billets, 2 O.R. to B/83 for Fatigues	
"	13/10/17		Cleaning Billets Improvement of Billets, remainder on Fatigues, Gun cleaning ect.	
"	14/10/17		2 O.R. Returned from C/83, remainder on fatigues, Gun cleaning ect.	
"	15/10/17		4 O.R. to A/83 for Fatigues. Remainder Gun cleaning	28
"	16/10/17		3 O.R. to A/83 for Fatigues. Do	

Army Form C. 2118.

WAR DIARY
or
INTELLIGENCE SUMMARY.

1/1 8 T.M. Battery

(Erase heading not required.)

Instructions regarding War Diaries and Intelligence Summaries are contained in F. S. Regs., Part II. and the Staff Manual respectively. Title pages will be prepared in manuscript.

Place	Date	Hour	Summary of Events and Information	Remarks and references to Appendices
In the Field	17-10-17		3 O.R. to B/83 for Fatigues. Remainder Gun Cleaning ect.	
	18-10-17		Do	
	19-10-17		3 O.R. returned from B/83. 2 O.R. to D/83 Bde for Fatigues. Remainder Battery Fatigues	
	20-10-17		2 O.R. to D/83 for Fatigues. Remainder Gun Cleaning and Fatigues	
	21-10-17		Do	
	22-10-17		2 O.R. Temporarily attd. to D/83 remainder on Fatigues and Gun Cleaning	
	23-10-17		Battery Fatigues and Gun Cleaning	
	24-10-17		4 O.R. returned from A.R.P. 5 O.R. Temporarily attached to C/82 for Fatigues	
	25-10-17		Battery Fatigues and Gun Cleaning. Inspection of gun appliances	
	26-10-17		O.C. Battery to D/82. Wagon line for Battery. Temporarily attached.	
	27-10-17		Battery Fatigues and Inspection	
	28-10-17		Do	
	29-10-17		Do	10.R. Returned from A.R.P.
	30-10-17		1 O.R. KILLED IN ACTION with D/82 Bde R.F.A.	
	31-10-17		Battery Fatigues, and Gun Cleaning	

W. Good Capt.
For O.C. 1/18 Trench Mortar Battery

Army Form C. 2118.

WAR DIARY
of
INTELLIGENCE SUMMARY.
(Erase heading not required.)

Instructions regarding War Diaries and Intelligence Summaries are contained in F. S. Regs., Part II. and the Staff Manual respectively. Title pages will be prepared in manuscript.

Y/18 J.M. BG

Place	Date	Hour	Summary of Events and Information	Remarks and references to Appendices
Shelton Bas Ypres Tours	November 1st		Officer, 2 O.R.s attached to Zonnar Dump at R.E. 4 O.R.s attached to 82nd Bde. 3 O.R.s attached to 82nd Bde.	
	2nd		"	"
	3rd		"	"
	4th		"	"
	5th		"	"
	6th		1 man attached to 1st 2 Division D.A.C. for signalling course	"
	7th		"	"
	8th		"	"
	9th		"	"
	10th		"	"
	11th		"	"
	12th		"	"
	13th		"	"
	14th		1 man attached to be hay of party	"
	15th		"	"
	16th		"	"
	17th		"	"
	18th		"	"
	19th		"	"
	20th		2 I.C.B. attached I officer school of Instruction	"

Army Form C. 2118.

WAR DIARY
or
INTELLIGENCE SUMMARY.
(Erase heading not required.)

Instructions regarding War Diaries and Intelligence Summaries are contained in F. S. Regs., Part II. and the Staff Manual respectively. Title pages will be prepared in manuscript.

Place	Date	Hour	Summary of Events and Information	Remarks and references to Appendices
Chateau Bec mont Huon	November 1914			
	21st		1 Officer 2 O.R.s attached Zouave Camp R.E. 4 O.R.s attached to 682nd Bde. 2 of P.E.s attached 5th Army School of Mortars. 3 O.R.s joined D 83rd Bde.	
	22nd		" "	
	23rd		" "	
	24th		" "	
	25th		" "	
	26th		" "	
	27th		4 O.R.s attached salvaging party	
	28th		1 O.R. returned from Zouave Camp R.E.	
	29th		1 O.R. attached Zouave Camp R.E. 5 O.R.s attached to salvaging party	
			3 O.R.s joined D 83rd Bde. 2 of P.E.s attached 5th Army School of Mortars	
	30th		2 O.R.s joined Salvage party	

Dinuber 6.23
G.L.
Z 18 J. M. Battery R.A.

Army Form C. 2118.

WAR DIARY
or
INTELLIGENCE SUMMARY.

(Erase heading not required.)

Instructions regarding War Diaries and Intelligence Summaries are contained in F. S. Regs., Part II. and the Staff Manual respectively. Title pages will be prepared in manuscript.

Place	Date	Hour	Summary of Events and Information	Remarks and references to Appendices
In the Field	1.12.17		J.O.R. in Fatigues for D Battery 13th Bde. R.F.A. Nucuvanedir on salvage work	
"	2.12.17		Do	
"	3.12.17		Do	
"	4.12.17		Do	
"	5.12.17		Do	
"	6.12.17		Do	
"	7.12.17		Do	
"	8.12.17		Do	
"	9.12.17		Do	
"	10.12.17		All ranks returned to Unit	
"	11.12.17		Inspection and Battery Fatigues	
"	12.12.17		Battery Turnout and Horse inspect	
"	13.12.17		Battery Inspection and Fatigues	
"	14.12.17		Reinstallation of personal marching Drill	
"	15.12.17		Dismty, Gun Guards Inspection of SBR's and 24 Salute Drill. 10.45 to 12.15 Gun Drill	
"	16.12.17		7.30 am Physical Training, Gun Parade with Arms 9.45am. 11.0 Gun Drill	
"	17.12.17		10.15 am Rifle and Foot Drill, 10.45am Mounted Drill	
"	18.12.17		7.30 am Physical Training 9.30 am Dism Parade with Arms 9.45 to 11.15. Foot Parade	

Army Form C. 2118.

WAR DIARY
or
INTELLIGENCE SUMMARY.
(Erase heading not required.)

Instructions regarding War Diaries and Intelligence Summaries are contained in F. S. Regs., Part II. and the Staff Manual respectively. Title pages will be prepared in manuscript.

Place	Date	Hour	Summary of Events and Information	Remarks and references to Appendices
In the Field	19.12.17	7.30 am	Physical Training. 9.00 Dress Parade with Arms. 9.45 Marching Drill. 10.30 Rifle Drill	
		11.15 am to 12.15 pm	Gun Drill.	
	20.12.17	7.30 am	Physical Training, 9.30 am Dress Parade, 9.45 am to 11.15 Route March 11.15 to 12.15 pm Gun Drill.	
	21.12.17	7.30 am	Physical Training 9.30 Dress Parade with Arms, 9.45 to 12.15 Route March.	
	22.12.17	7.30 am	Physical Training, 9.30 Dress Parade with Arms 9.45 to 11.45 Marching Drill, 2.0 pm Foot Inspection, 12.15 D.T.M.O. Inspection of Billets. 2.30 Bathing Parade.	
	23.12.17	9.30	Dress Parade with Arms.	
	24.12.17	7.30	Physical Training 9.30 Dress Parade, S.B.R. & P.H. Helmet Drill 10.45 to 11.45 am	
			Gun Drill, 11.45 to 12.15 Lecture on Gunn.	
	25.12.17	10 am	Dress Parade	
	26.12.17	9.30	Dress Parade	
	27.12.17	7.30 am	Physical Training 9.30 am Dress Parade with Arms, 9.45 Marching Drill.	
		10.30 am to 11.30 am	Gun Drill. 11.30 to 12.15 Lecture on Gunn.	
	28.12.17	7.30 am	Physical Training, 9.30 am Dress Parade 9.45 Marching Drill, 10.30 Gun Drill.	
			(11 mins with S.B.Rs respirators) 11.45 to 12.15 Lecture on Gunn.	
	29.12.17	7.30 am	Physical Training 9.45 Marching Drill, 10.45 to 11.45 Gun Drill 12.0 noon HS	
			Respirators, 12.15 pm Inspection of Billets by D.T.M.O. 2.30 pm Bathing Parade	
	30.12.17	9.30	Dress Parade. 9.45 Church Parade for noncomformists 10.0 am R.C. Church Parade.	
	31.12.17	7.30 am	Physical Training 9.30 Dress Parade. 9.45 Battery Fatigues	

Army Form C. 2118.

WAR DIARY
INTELLIGENCE SUMMARY.
(Erase heading not required.)

January 1918

Place	Date	Hour	Summary of Events and Information	Remarks and references to Appendices
CROMBEKE	1st		Battery moved by lorries to LARREY FARM, ELVERDINGHE (Sheet 28 NW B.9.C.14)	
B.9.C.14	1-4th		1 N.C.O. + 3 men attached LUNAVILLE DUMP	
"	5th-31st		1 N.C.O. + 4 men at STRAY FARM Salvaging Ammunition	
"	21st-24th		Four other ranks attached 18th Divl Art H.Q.	

W. Good Lieut R.G.A.
of O.C. Y/18 Im. By

Y/18 T.M.B. R.A.

FEBRUARY 1918

WAR DIARY
or
INTELLIGENCE SUMMARY
(Erase heading not required.)

Army Form C. 2118

Place	Date Feb	Hour	Summary of Events and Information	Remarks and references to Appendices
ELVERDINGHE	1st		Battery entrained to go to #Army T.M. School.	
"	2nd	9.0 A.M	2/Lt. A.E. Vaudin. M.C. (RFA (T/c.) & 2/Lt. K.E.R. RFA. and 23. O.R. left ELVERDINGHE for Poperinghe	
POPERINGHE	"	11.30AM	POPERINGHE. Left POPERINGHE for AMIENS by rail	
AMIENS	3rd	6.36 A.M	Arrived AMIENS	
AMIENS	"	2.0 P.M	Left by lorry for T.M. School. + Arm. VAUX-EN-AMIENOIS. Arrd. VAUX 3.45 p.m.	
VAUX-EN-AMIENOIS	4th		Battery on 2nd/y Course of Instruction on 6" T. Howr.	
"	to 19th			
"	19th	6.30AM	Left School by Lorry for AMIENS.	
AMIENS	19th		Stayed night 19th–20th at Rest Camp. AMIENS.	
"	20th	6.22AM	Left AMIENS by Rail 5.22 A.M. for FLAVY-LE-MARTEL and. FLAVY. 12.0 noon	
FLAVY-LE-MARTEL	21st		Left FLAVY. to. Known area of BENAY (Sheet 66 c. N.W. A21 a. 2. 5)	
			Arrived BENAY. 4.30 p.m.	
BENAY	22nd to 28th		Battery employed in building down 6" T.M. Emplacements in Back Line. Four Pits at BENAY (Sh. 66 c. N.W. A 21 a central) three at ADOLPHE POST (H 33. c. central)	
			As the T.M. Battery numbered a re-organisation resulted & the Battery was on the Sergt., the R.G.A. Personnel returning with Y/18. we is to CLIFFORD CAMP. nr POPERINGHE. to join II Corps Heavy Battery. i.e. VIII. H.T.M.B. J.R./F/A Personnel of Jt. X. Y. & Z /18 Batteries were formed into two 6 gun 6" Batteries and re-armed with 6" T. Howr. instead of 2" T. Howr.	

H Vaudin Lt. RFA (F)
for o/c Y/18 T.M.B. R.A.
28/2/18.

18th Div.

WAR DIARY

Y/18 TRENCH MORTAR BATTERY, R.A.

MARCH

1918

Army Form C. 2118

WAR DIARY or INTELLIGENCE SUMMARY
(Erase heading not required.)

Instructions regarding War Diaries and Intelligence Summaries are contained in F.S. Regs., Part II. and the Staff Manual respectively. Title Pages will be prepared in manuscript.

Hqrs 2 R.A.   MARCH 1918

Place	Date	Hour	Summary of Events and Information	Remarks and references to Appendices
REMIGNY	8th		Two Sections completed and guns mis attached to 117th Div. Arty at BENAY (M21C). Remaining Sections was employed on general fatigues.	Maps: Sheet 66 D N.W. (Benay Section) Sheet 66 D N.W. Edition 2A (Guinguette Section)
	9th		Capts. F.W. McCombie and Wilson Elliott together rode to this sector behind Line 3rd Army Shrivel Number Scheme.	
	10th		Reconnaissance was carried out to select sites for T.M. positions near GUINGUETTE FARM.	
	11th		Gun emplacements were marked out and lines of fire laid. Arrangements for works completed.	
	12th-14th		Work was commenced at "W36 A05.65". Gun emplacements drive carried out daily.	
	19th		One mobile emplacement completed and mortar moved up into. Ammunition refuses and communication trenches completed.	
	20th		A fair proportion of roads and paths done to day on the Second supplemental. Ammo 200 rounds ammunition stored.	
	21st	4:30am	German attack began with a heavy bombardment into half N.E. and gas Shells. A heavy mist described preventing the morning. Owing to the great reduction to fire zone not follow until about 9am as no communication from the forward area had been received. In consequence about 25% only of the available ammunition had been expended when the guns detachments found they were surrounded by the Enemy. Before making their escape however, the guns were rendered useless. Definite details of all casualties is not yet known.	
VILLEQUIER AUMONT	22nd		Remaining Personnel from positions at BENAY & GUINGUETTE FARM attached to N21, Siu DAC.	
	31st			

Signed W.H.
Capt. R.A.
OC 2/1st T.M.B. R.A.

18th Div.

Y/18 TRENCH MORTAR BATTERY, R.A.

A P R I L

1 9 1 8

Army Form C. 2118

WAR DIARY or **INTELLIGENCE SUMMARY**

(Erase heading not required.)

APRIL 1918   Y/187 T.M.B. R.A.

Instructions regarding War Diaries and Intelligence Summaries are contained in F.S. Regs., Part II. and the Staff Manual respectively. Title Pages will be prepared in manuscript.

Place	Date	Hour	Summary of Events and Information	Remarks and references to Appendices
End of month	1st to 7th		Battery attached to No.1. Section 18th D.A.C. during line of march.	
CHARNY	8th		Battery marched to CHARNY.	
"	9th		Inspection and General Fatigues.	
WARLUS	10th		Battery moved by lorries to WARLUS (Commune of TAILLY).	
GRANDFART	11th		" " " GRANDFART.	
"	12th to 14th		Daily parades, refitting and general fatigues.	
AMIENS	15th		Battery moved by lorries to AMIENS.	
BOVES	16th		" " " BOVES. 1 Officer and 18th A.R.P.	
"	17th		1 Officer and 26 O.R. at 18th A.R.P. Remaining personnel, general fatigues.	
"	18th		" " " " " " " "	
"	19th		" " " " " " " "	
"	20th		" " " " " " " "	
"	21st		" " " " " " " " Fatigue for 62nd Bde. N.A.	
"	22nd		" " " " " " " " "	
"	23rd		" " " " " " " " "	
"	24th		" " " " " " " " "	1 N.C.O. at III Corps Gas School
"	25th		" " " " " " " " "	"
"	26th		" " " " " " " " "	"
"	27th		" " " " " " " " "	1 Officer to 18th A.R.P.
"	28th		2 Officers and 25 O. Ranks returned from 18th A.R.P. Battery moved by lorries to held area at ST OUEN	returned from fatigue at 62nd Bde N.A. 1 N.C.O. returned from III Corps Gas School
"	29th		Inspection of box respirator kits.	
"	30th			

Alfred Smith
Capt R.A.
O.C. Y/18 T.M.B. R.A.

Army Form C. 2118.

WAR DIARY
or
INTELLIGENCE SUMMARY
(Erase heading not required.)

1/16 T.M.B. R.A.

MAY. 1916.

Ref: Map { Sheet 62 P.N.E. 1/20,000 }

Place	Date	Hour	Summary of Events and Information	Remarks and references to Appendices
ST OUEN	1st } 4th }		Daily inspection. Inspection of A.B.G and B.H. stink. Rifle stink. Physical and trenching drill. Stomopheu and Salute.	
BEHENCOURT	5th		Battery moved by lorries to BEHENCOURT.	
"	6th		Battery took over positions in the line from 31st Battery, 2nd Australian D.A. (positions in D.13, E.13, E.7, Sheet 62 NW (1/40,000)	
LINE.	7th		Intermediate extension in Syndication. Three new sites were taken over. Reason to sink new saline occupied was that shells in BAIZIEUX. Several ridges fire on Enfilade, and day work. Bn registration drill	
"	8th		40 A.M. Lieut. REED posted to 1/16 T.M.B. R.A. from 11th D.A.C.	
"	9th		As the register of the instructing the firing was done to day.	
"	10th		75 rounds expended on the following Corps G:- Hands (Mortar at E20 A59, Battery E14 C27 Enemy trenches from E14 A59.6 E14 A13.	
"	11th		No. 113977 Cpl Coghanduc & Systematic band admitted to C.C.S. (Puits). Open approach track.	
"	"		No. 77238 Cpl Maclerglow D. Systematic band admitted to C.C.S.	
"	"		50 rounds expended on the following Corps G:- Hands Mortar E14 A59.	
"	12th		90 " " " " " " " Hands Mortar E14 A59, Hands Mortar E14 C49, Hands Mortar Guns E14 C31, Sniper E13 B94, Enemy E14 Q	
"	13th		65 " " " " " " " Hands Mortar E14 A59. Hands Mortar E14 A13. Battle hand into line E13 D00.15 to E13 D30.60	
"	14th		90 " " " " " " " Hands Mortar E14 A59. Battle hand into line E13 D00.10 to C. E14 A43	
"	15th		90 " " " " " " " * Mine ENewy trenches from E13 D22 to E13 D70.00 * Mine Sickey trenches from E13 D10.35. E13 B.10.00 to E14 A00.20 and	
"	16th		90 " " " " " " " E14 A00.20.15 E14 A10.45 ditto	
"	17th		190 " " " " " " " Mine E13 D00.15 to E13 D60.70. E13 B9.00 to E14 A00.15. E14 A5.30 to E14 A35.70.	
"	18th		150 " " " " " " " 8 gunners posted to 1/16 T.M.B. R.A. from 11th D.A.C.	
			Enemy Farrold line in E14 A in Accordance with Artillery Programme. Nighte of Haj. Battalion Officer	
				* Enquiry by reason of G.O.C. 53 Inf Bde.
				Bn Vick. SOS. ANCLE.

WAR DIARY or INTELLIGENCE SUMMARY

Army Form C. 2118.

1/8 TN B RA

MAY 1917

Place	Date	Hour	Summary of Events and Information	Remarks and references to Appendices
L.11.C	19th		No firing today. Glass today.	
"	20th	72 rounds B.L.bullets on the following targets:- Silung Opens E14 A99, tracks on E14.B, Mtn Gunny tracks from E13.D20 to E13.D30	
"	21st	60	Dump E14 C37, Sunken Road E14 C09, Gnb E14 A71	
"	22nd	60	"	
"	23rd	60	Valley E14 A, x.Roads E13 D55	
"	24th	65	Tanks and carts visible E13 D.20. Machine guns E14 C37. Enemy heavily harassed our own support line	
"	25th	21	Dumps North E14 C19, tracks from _____ E14 C37	
"	"	5	15 shots on M62 Trench line was destroyed. Direct hit on dugout	
"	26th	60	Machine Guns E14 A42. Direct Myler E14 A13. Enemy transports E14 C70 B E14 C64	
"	"	7	M.22.070 Serge Taylor 2/C. wounded and admitted to C.C.S.	
"	27th	60	Shots on new E14 B20 and E13 B90. No firing reported from	
"	"	1	Show on new E14 B20. One Gun as reported by 4TH M.G.H.Gun Div. 1/3 DAG.	
"	28th		E14 C52-16 E14 B1 90.	
"	29th		No firing took place today. General fatigues on emplacements done today.	
			Handed over to 41st Divisional Trench Mortar Batteries.	
BAIZEUX			During the period in action the Batteries did good service. Direct hits (details are always done not knowing this form	
			be certain) frequently the men put our aspects had considerable damage were caused being much fired on rather no shots	
			the foremost at Lights Authority to. Many instances firing was carried out in construction with Sister Batteries with excellent effect.	
	30th		Guns next from 4th Div. Trench Mortar Batteries handed over to HEYENCOURT WOOD (Valable was positions as K26 D56 & K31 D.60.5)	
"	31st		Inspection of Gears Equipment the day. Guns now resting.	

Signed

OC, 1/8 TN B RA

Army Form C. 2118.

Instructions regarding War Diaries and Intelligence Summaries are contained in F. S. Regs., Part II and the Staff Manual respectively. Title pages will be prepared in manuscript.

WAR DIARY
or
INTELLIGENCE SUMMARY.
(Erase heading not required.)

1/87 M.B. R.A.   JUNE 1918.

Ref: Map: SENLIS Sheet 57D S.E. 20,000
and Sheet 57D S.E. 10,500

Place	Date	Hour	Summary of Events and Information	Remarks and references to Appendices
BAIZIEUX	1st		Work carried out on positions in HENENCOURT WOOD.	
"	2nd		" " " " " " " " " "	
"	3rd		Inspection of arms and equipment. Gun Drill B.R. drill, Physical and rifle drill.	
LINE	4th		Battery took over positions in the line from 58th Divl. Trench Mortars. (Map Ref: 57D S.E.)	
"	5th		Registered Quarry Map C.27 Road North at W21.D.17 with 16 Rounds. No rifle firing was done on account of infantry relief.	
"	"		Registered Quarry Map C.27 Road North at W21.D.17 with 16 Rounds.	
"	"		A total of 30 rounds were fired and covered the following points W21.D.13, W21.B.94, W21.D.47, W21.A.5.60.	
"	6th		N° 70619 Gr. (Sig/Br.) Morrison C.D. wounded and admitted to C.C.S.	
"	"		Expended 40 rounds the enemy front line was at W15.D.35.65 and eastwards for 25x. Four positions dug & accessible, making for wire cutting.	
"	7th		Expended 20 rounds our Forward Gun Line was at W21.B.99.72. Sub-area two mortars were brought up into position nearly completed.	
"	"		Enemy heavily bombarded our left front between 9.15pm and 10.45pm. No action followed.	
"	8th		1/18 T.M.B. R.A. Relieved by 4/19 T.M.B. R.A. Battery took over positions in LA HAZE V21.D. During the few days in the line, a	
"	"		Considerable amount of work was done on the positions and dugouts were made and practically completed before relief. Remainder of battery returned to BAIZIEUX on relief.	
BAIZIEUX	8th 9th		1 Officer and 10 O. Ranks at MILLENCOURT in charge of mortars at Brown position.	
"	9th		Lectures, fatigues and inspection of arms and equipment.	
"	10th		Inspection. Gun Drill B.R. drill, Rifle and Machine drill.	
"	11th		" " " " " " " Lecture - Discipline.	
LINE	12th		1/18 T.M.B. R.A. relieved 4/19 T.M.B. R.A. in the line. Expended 25 rounds on enemy front line trench at W15.D.50.15 to W15.D.65.00	
"	"		During the night testing disposed is shells were put in the following target W27.B.39.72. (Machine Gun) W27.B.35.40 (Trench Mortar).	
"	13th		No firing took place to-day. No night firing took place on account of our patrol activity.	
"	14th		Expended 60 rounds on enemy front line near at N21.B.65.75. No night firing on account of our patrol activity.	
"	"		10 Reinforcements joined from 1st DAC.	

Army Form C. 2118.

Instructions regarding War Diaries and Intelligence
Summaries are contained in F. S. Regs., Part II.
and the Staff Manual respectively. Title pages
will be prepared in manuscript.

WAR DIARY
or
INTELLIGENCE SUMMARY

(Erase heading not required.)

1/18 Tn. B. Ry.   JUNE 1918.

Place	Date	Hour	Summary of Events and Information	Remarks and references to Appendices
LINE	16th		Explosive 20 rounds on Enemy Front line at W21.D.80.58. 43 rifle firing in support of Patrol activity.	
"	10th		1/18 Tn.B.Ry. relieved by 4/18 Tn.B. Ry. Gallery returned to billets in BAIZIEUX	
BAIZIEUX	17th		Inspections. Gen. Drill, B.R. and rifle drill. Laying out new lines of fire in preparation of ammunition.	
"	18th		Cleaning continued — the following Lectures were included. Gun Drill, Laying, B.R. drill, fuzes, instructions. Lectures on B.R.'s to T.M.'s	
"	19th		"	
LINE	20th	{ Gun Drill. Gas alert Instructions. History of T.M. Explosives. Lectures on ammunition. Care and preservation of ammunition.	
"		1/18 Tn.B.Ry. relieved 4/18 Tn.B. Ry. in the line.		
"	21st		Wire cutting tasks were continued. (W21.D.68 and W21.D.2.) Work on dugouts carried out at night.	
"	22nd		(W21.D.20.82.) (W21.D.30.90) 10 rounds expelled on Enemy T.M. at W21.A.6.15.	
"	23rd		Total of 110 rounds were expelled on the following targets. Wire and front line W21.D.25 to W21.D28 and Trench W21.D.95.13 to W21.A.10.55"	
"	24th		No firing took place to day. Work on new emplacements and on dugouts was carried out. 1/18 Tn.B.Ry. relieved by 4/18 Tn.B Ry. Gallery returned to billets in BAIZIEUX	
BAIZIEUX	25th		Inspection. General Cleanup.	
"	26th		Morning Parade in accordance with programme.	
"	27th		"	
"	28th		"	
LINE	29th		1/18 Tn.B. Ry relieved 4/18 Tn.B. Ry. in the line. 181 rounds expelled on Enemy front line and Trench Mortars.	
"	30th		Reported Disposals to Battery Hd. Qrs. Gallery standing by. 54th Infantry Brigade. Wires were cut to capture to Enemy front line. The telephone was succesful. S.O.S. tasks was made and testing rendered. Support by firing on this S.O.S. lines	

30/6/18

Signed
OC 1/18 Tn.B. Ca Corps R.A

18th DIVISION.
ARTILLERY

Y/18 TRENCH MORTAR BATTERY

AUGUST 1918

Army Form C. 2118.

WAR DIARY
or INTELLIGENCE SUMMARY

1/18 T.M.B. R.A.

AUGUST 1918

(Erase heading not required.)

Place	Date	Hour	Summary of Events and Information	Remarks and references to Appendices
BERTRICOURT	1st		Training continued and carried out in accordance with Programmes. D.T.M.'s O.O. 1/16 Issued re to HEILLY and for carrying out a reconnaissance of system to be handed over. Arrangements for relief completed. (Major. Fairhurst and S.2.R N.E.)	
HEILLY	2nd		Battery moved by lorries to HEILLY (near M.R.) and relieved 10th Wiltshires M.T.B. Battery. Section H.Q. 6/6 Trek hrs taken over & O.Ps. and positions in the line. One mortar was landed over, line of which are in reserve positions. Incoming personnel had no active ???? [re] at rear H.Q. HEILLY.	
LINE	3rd		Work on Positions was commenced. Immediate Schemes to engage any target the indicating may call for shot to be no readiness to assume S.O.S. Calls.	
"	4th		Mortar and positions at K.1.D.20.65. landed over to 1/25 M.T.M. Battery. A new site was reconnoitred and chosen at K.13.B.12.00 1/25 T.M. Btty landed over mortars and deep dugouts in exchange.	
"	5th		Work on positions continued. Expended 4 rounds to verify registrations.	
"	6th		Mortars and positions at K.19.C.50.22 and K.13.C.55.10. were taken over from 1/50 Dist. Trench Mortars. One mortar and 1 G.S. Bin and 1 Supp. Bin landed over to 1/50 Dist Trench Mortars.	
"	7th		Great enemy activity. Neus routine attack by him resulted in his temporary possession of Reiv Mortars.	
"	8th		At 4.20 a.m. the division attacked. Mortars now registered and later were used ??? and brought back to rear H.Q. HEILLY. All mortars with the exception of a front at 7ths Relief. Returned to Rear HEILLY. General Bagarre and few casualties. Make.	
HEILLY	9th		Ground at 782.30 relieved by 4/18 T.M.B. R.A. Chatsp [party] detailed to convert Rifle Grade P.F.A. Mess Cart from forwards	
"	10th		General Fatigue.	
"	11th			
"	12th		1st ???? ???? Do this party detailed [for] ???? tow ???? (at HEILLY).	

A5834 Wt. W4973/M687 750,000 8/16 D. D. & L. Ltd. Forms/C.2118/13.

Army Form C. 2118.

WAR DIARY
or
INTELLIGENCE SUMMARY. 1/15 TM B. RA

(Erase heading not required.)

Instructions regarding War Diaries and Intelligence Summaries are contained in F. S. Regs., Part II. and the Staff Manual respectively. Title pages will be prepared in manuscript.

AUGUST 1918.

Place	Date	Hour	Summary of Events and Information	Remarks and references to Appendices
HÉILLY	13th	-	Ammunition taken from positions and Stables ready for removal.	
"	14th	-	Inspection of Arms and Equipment.	
"	15th	-	No. 66534 L/C Tolson proceeded to England for tour of home duty. General Fatigues	
"	"	-	Ammunition Stables ready for removal on 15th.	
"	16th	-	1 Officer and 20 other ranks at Dump (HÉILLY). Collecting and dumping at A.R.P. TREUX.	
"	20th	-	"	Remaining personnel on fatigue
"	21st	-	1 Officer and 15 other ranks at Dump at T32A (See 62nd Divn Edition I)	
"	"	-	1 " " 30 " " " " HÉILLY. Remaining General on fatigue.	
"	22nd	-	"	
"	23rd	-	"	
"	24th	-	"	
"	25th	-	"	
"	26th	-	1 Officer and 10 other ranks withdrawn from Dump at T32A.	
"	27th	-	1 " " 20 " " " HÉILLY.	
"	28th	-	1 " " 20 " " " provides for Dumps at FRICOURT. (Sheet 62D Sevid Edition I).	
E.6.C.4.4.	29th	-	Battery marches from HÉILLY to E.6.C.4.4. (Sheet 62D Sevid Edition I).	
"	29th	-	Remaining personnel engaged on taking Rotary T.M. & Ammunition Stables Area to enemy's Operning line Country.	
"	30th	-	"	"
MONTALBAN	31st	-	Marched to New Hampshire billets at Montalban.	"

O.C. 1/15 TM B RA.

Army Form C. 2118.

WAR DIARY
or
INTELLIGENCE SUMMARY.

(Erase heading not required.)

Y/15 T.M.B. R.A.

SEPTEMBER 1918

Place	Date	Hour	Summary of Events and Information	Remarks and references to Appendices
MONTAUBAN	1st		1 Officer and 20 Other Ranks for Ammunition dumps. Ordinary general fatigues on fatigues for 62nd Brigade R.F.A.	
"	2nd		"	
"	3rd		"	
"	4th		"	
PRIEZ FARM	5th		Ordinary general fatigues to and attached billet at PRIEZ FARM. General fatigues.	
"	6th		10 Other ranks on Ammunition dumps.	
"	7th		"	
"	8th		1 Officer & 18 Other ranks took mobile T.M. forward under orders of 12th D.A.	
"	9th		1 Officer & 14 Other ranks with mobile T.M. acting under orders from 63rd D.A.	
"	"		Remainder personnel moved by lorry to LIBRAMONT.	
LIBRAMONT	10th		1 Officer and 10 other ranks at Ammunition dumps. 1 Officer and 18 other ranks with mobile T.M. acting under orders from 58 D.A.	
"	11th		" One mobile mortar taken forward and placed in position.	
"	12th		" Second mobile mortar taken forward and placed in position. 50 rounds expended during rifle harassing fire.	
"	13th		"	
"	14th		"	
"	15th		"	
"	16th		" Two more mortars taken forward and placed in position. 120 rounds expended during night harassing fire.	
"	17th		" Troops attacked to occupy a position overlooking the HINDENBURG LINE. 50 rounds expended in support of the attack.	
"	18th		Mortars withdrawn and brought back to LIBRAMONT. Personnel returned to LIBRAMONT.	

A 5834 Wt. W4973/M687 750,000 8/16 D. D. & L. Ltd. Forms/C.2118/13.

Army Form C. 2118

WAR DIARY or INTELLIGENCE SUMMARY.

(Erase heading not required.)

SEPTEMBER 1918.   Y/18 T.M.B. R.A.

Instructions regarding War Diaries and Intelligence Summaries are contained in F. S. Regs., Part II. and the Staff Manual respectively. Title pages will be prepared in manuscript.

Place	Date	Hour	Summary of Events and Information	Remarks and references to Appendices
LIÉRAMONT	19th		Battery rejoined the division. 1 Officer & 10 Other Ranks to Ammunition dump.	
"			Inspection parade, arms and equipment. Gun cleaning and general fatigue.	
"	20th		One detachment together with one detachment of Y/14 took forward two mortars and took up position at F.16.A.1.3. (Sheet 62t NE).	
"			Expended 53 rounds on "X" "Y" and "Z" Copses in F.16.B.D. and F.1.C, after which infantry carried out a silent penetration and occupied these copses.	
"	21st		Expended 103 rounds on targets selected by B.C. commanding 52nd Infantry Brigade, in support of infantry attack.	
"	22nd		Mortars moved to a forward position in order to engage TEMBOIS Fm. and E.G4 B.S.T.	
"	23rd		Registered TEMBOIS Fm. and E.G6 P.O.S.T.	
"	24th		Expended 57 rounds in support of an infantry attack on these points.	
"			Mortars were withdrawn this evening and brought back to LIÉRAMONT. Opponents retreated to their rear lines at LIÉRAMONT.	
"	25th		Inspection of arms and equipment. Gas respirator drill. 1 Officer and 10 Other Ranks returned from Ammunition dump.	
"	26th		Inspection. Gun drill and laying drill.	
"	27th		1 Officer and 21 Other Ranks left for Fifth Army Trench Mortar School.	
"			5 Other Ranks sent to assist at Ammunition dump.	
"	28th		Rifle and revolver drill and Semaphore.	
"	29th		General fatigue.	
"	30th		Inspection of Gas Respirators and B.R. drill. One detachment together with one detachment of Y/14 took forward two mortars to LEMPIRE, with a view to taking up position later, to engage the hostile defences W. of VENDHUILLE.	
"			13th Division captured VENDHUILLE to-day and told the line of the Canal, N. and E. of the Village. 5 Other Ranks returned from dump.	

Sept 30th 1918.

A. M. Marsh Capt. R.A.
O.C. Y/18 T.M.B. R.A.

A5834 Wt. W4973/M687 750,000 8/16 D.D. & L. Ltd. Forms/C.2118/13.

WAR DIARY or INTELLIGENCE SUMMARY

Army Form C. 2118.

Y/18 Trench Mortar Bty R.A.   Ref. Maps Sheet 62c ⅟₂₀,₀₀₀

Place	Date	Hour	Summary of Events and Information	Remarks and references to Appendices
LIERAMONT	Oct 1st - 8th		Battery concentrated at LIERAMONT. 10 men on Dvn A.R.P. PEZIERES [62c]	
LEMPIRE	Oct 3rd		Capt. F.H. McCOMBIE, O.C battery, proceeded on leave 6/10/18 - 23/10/18.	
SERAIN	Oct 9th		Moved to LEMPIRE. Mortars & temp. surplus stores dumped at LIERAMONT under guard.	
	Oct 10th		Division continued its advance and battery moved to SERAIN. [57B]	
BERTRY	" 11th		Battery moved to BERTRY [57B] Bn. A.R.P. established at BERTRY and remaining personnel of battery	
	1st Oct 18th		attached trench mortar duty.	
	Oct 21st		Orders received 10.90. into action E.f LE CATEAU [57J] to support attack. Positions allocated at K35.6.03 [57B] mortars & ammunition issued up.	
	" 22nd		Orders to go into action cancelled. Battery moved to REUMONT [57J] Mortars arrived at battery.	
LE CATEAU	" 23rd		Division attacked. Battery moved into LE CATEAU	
	" 25th		Capt. F.H. McCOMBIE returned from leave & resumed command of battery. 2/Lieut G.R. THOMSON posted to A/83 R.F.A.	
	" 27th		Maj. Battery taken 4 mobile mortars into action.	
	" 28th		Mortars taken up positions in F.24.C and are registered.	
	" 29th		Targets engaged at request of Inf. Bde. 150 Rounds expended. Battery H.Q. at BOUSIES [57J]	
	" 30th		One section advanced to A.19.d. and registered. Inf. Bde targets again engaged. 275 rounds expended.	
	31st		1235 Rounds expended.	
			The battery has had 3 bg. The casualties during the month — 1 O.R. wounds — 2 wounded (gas). It has been abundantly proved in the operations of the past month that as long as a T.M. Battery is w/Horst Transport stores and have to rely on that obtained from the D.A.C for animals the supply and working of mortars it cannot be relied upon as a mobile unit. O.T.M. battery will suffer sufficient transport to make its self contained is some respect would be of great assistance to the infantry in warfare such as the Division has experienced during the month.	

Dilwuluke S. Capt.
K. Y/18 T.M.B. RA.

Dated 31 Aug

Army Form C. 2118.

WAR DIARY
or
INTELLIGENCE SUMMARY.

Y/19 TRENCH MORTAR BATTERY R.A.
Sheet 57A N.W.
REF: MAPS. 57D N.E.

NOVEMBER, 1918.

(Erase heading not required.)

Place	Date	Hour	Summary of Events and Information	Remarks and references to Appendices
LE CATEAU	1st		100 rounds expended on enemy at A20 C35 & A20 C&5 with excellent results. Several shoots hits were observed. Fire was opened on two tanks at ridges of infantry into reported that they penetrated machine guns. A further 160 rounds were fired on the "Triangle." (A20 C & D).	Capt. Clark
"	2nd		160 rounds expended on the "Triangle". One section advanced to A19 D, and registered	Capt. Clark
BOUSIES	3rd		Battery moved to BOUSIES. Visual cavalry engaged. Visits to positions was carried out today in view of impending attack. Battery	
"	4th		Division attacked. 200 rounds expended on "Triangle" (roads known to be in A20 C & D) in support of this attack. Mortars were withdrawn and together with the 4th Remaining rounds of ammunition, was dumped at A19 D 32, and a guard mounted.	
"	5th		Remaining personnel returned to BOUSIES. (No suffered no casualties during the operation).	Capt. Clark
"	6th		Beds were returned for repair. Guns and 5800 rounds back to BOUSIES and remaining ammunition returned to A.R.P.	
"	"		One section detailed to relieve section of X/18 T.M.B. R.A. who had been following up the infantry during their advance.	
"	"		Munitions were withdrawn battalion who stated they expected to be withdrawn this afternoon. At 1530 hours orders received through 55th Infantry Bde to withdraw and return to BOUSIES.	Capt. Clark
"	7th		Battery rested and refitted. General fatigues.	Capt. Clark
"	8th		Battery marched to read billets at MARETZ. Division in Corps reserve.	
MARETZ	9th		Inspection on respirators, box respirators and remaining equipment. Gun cleaning and general fatigues.	Capt. Clark
"	10th			
"	12th		Inspection of arms, Gun cleaning and general fatigues.	
"	13th			
"	19th		Battery inspected by Lt Colonel Dr. Selway "CMG", particular attention being given to T.M. ammunition orders issued by Divisions - Working in connection with the 5th Lt T.M. Battery — Here Bank Bombs are collected and stopped on in accordance with D...	Capt. Clark

Under O.C. Y/19 T.M.B. R.A. who is responsible that all Bombs not Fuzees Back Bombs are collected and stored up in accordance with D...
instructions issued by Divisions
A5834 Wt. W4973/M687 750,000 8/16 D.D. & L. Ltd. Forms/C.2113/13.

Army Form C. 2118.

WAR DIARY
or
INTELLIGENCE SUMMARY.

1/1 ST TRENCH MORTAR BATTERY. R.A

(Erase heading not required.)

Instructions regarding War Diaries and Intelligence Summaries are contained in F. S. Regs., Part II. and the Staff Manual respectively. Title pages will be prepared in manuscript.

NOVEMBER 1918

Place	Date	Hour	Summary of Events and Information	Remarks and references to Appendices
MARETZ	20 } 23 }		Battery Employed on Salvage work under orders issued by Division	Fine
"	24		Salvage work completed. Church and inspection parades and recreation	Dull
"	25		Inspection parade. Gun cleaning, parades fatigues and recreation	Fine
"	26			Fine
"	30		Inspection parade. Educational training, recreation and general fatigues	Fine
			G Downing Lieut. this month the battery has suffered no battle casualties	

November 30th 1918.

D.Armstrong. Capt. R.A.
O.C. 1/1st T.M.B. R.A

Army Form C. 2118.

WAR DIARY
or
INTELLIGENCE SUMMARY

Army Form C. 2118.

1/8 Trench Mortar Battery R.A.

Ref Map { Valenciennes }

(Erase heading not required.)

Place	Date	Hour	Summary of Events and Information	Remarks and references to Appendices
MAUBEUGE	1st–4th		Inspection parades. Educational training. Recreation and General fatigues.	
"	5th		Gallery. Employed on Salvage work under orders of 54th Infantry Brigade.	
"	5th		No 70519 Gr Manions C.B. posted to Transportation Depot, Base Depot, Calais.	
"	6th/9th		Inspection parades. Educational training. Recreation and General fatigues.	
"	8th		No 94286. Bomb. Mitchelson A. to 7th Army Musso Training centre (to be passed constructor).	
"	10th		No 73264 Bomb. Coulston E.H.	
"	10th		No 62205 A/Cpl S. Williamson J.	
"	10th		No 94259 Gr Cain T.	
"	10th		No 13 Gr Jones E.G.	
"	10th		No 20110 DR (Signaller) Whitlock S.A.	
"	11th		Inspection parade. Educational training. Recreation and General fatigues.	
"	12th		{ Officer "B" order Bomb moves to billets at ESNES for Salvage work under orders from 54th Inf. Bde.	
"	12th		{ Remaining personnel :- Educational training, parades, recreation and general fatigues.	
"	13th		" "	
"	14th		" "	
"	14th		Major Macloure R.F.A. left to proceed to England for employment on demobilization.	
"	15th		{ Officer "B" detachments at ESNES attached to 54th Inf Bde for Salvage work	
"	21st		{ Remaining personnel :- Educational training, parades, recreation and General fatigues.	

Army Form C. 2118.

WAR DIARY
or
INTELLIGENCE SUMMARY
(Erase heading not required.)

V/19 TRENCH MORTAR BATTERY R.A.

DECEMBER 1918.

Place	Date	Hour	Summary of Events and Information	Remarks and references to Appendices
MARETZ	22nd		1 Officer & 26 other ranks returned from ESNES.	
"			Remainder engaged :- Educational training, parades, recreation and general fatigues.	Copy.
"	23rd			
"	24th		Inspection parade, general fatigues and recreation.	Copy.
"	25th		Holiday!	Copy.
"	26th		{ 1 Officer & 26 other ranks proceeded to ESNES for the purpose of reaming the work of Salvage under orders of S.U. Inf. Bde. Hqrs.	Copy.
"			Remainder engaged :- General fatigues.	Copy.
"	27th			
"	6th		1 Officer & 26 other ranks at ESNES attached to S.U. Inf. Bde. for Salvage work.	Copy.
"	31st		Remainder engaged :- Educational training, parades, recreation & general fatigues.	Copy.

December 31st 1918.

[Signature]
Capt. R.A.
O.C. V/19 T.M.B. R.A.

WAR DIARY or **INTELLIGENCE SUMMARY**

Army Form C. 2118.

1/1st TRENCH MORTAR BATTERY R.A.

JANUARY 1919

Place	Date	Hour	Summary of Events and Information	Remarks and references to Appendices
MAGETZ	1st		Daily parades and inspections, Educational training, recreation and general fatigues.	
"	6th		(1 Officer and 28 O.Ranks at ESNES allotted to 5th Inf. Bde for Railway work.)	
"	15th			
"	16th		1 Officer and 26 O.Ranks returned to battery having completed railway work on their areas. (Auth: S.O. 1st Inf. Bde.)	
"	17th		Daily parades and inspections, Educational training, recreation and general fatigues.	
"	18th		"	
"	19th		"	N⁰ 71075 Corp. J. GIBB. T. To Enfield Branch. } Bmt
"	20th		"	
"	21st		"	
"	22nd		"	
"	23rd		"	N⁰ 753495 Gnr. W.E. KIDD. to Enfield Branch.
"	24th		"	N⁰ 103359 Bomb. COTTIS. J.W. to Enfield Branch. } Bmt
"	25th		- do -	
"	26th		- do -	N⁰ 411152 Gnr. G.F. McDONALD. L. to Enfield Branch.
"	27th		- do -	
"	29th		- do -	} Bmt
"	30th		- do -	
"	31st		Strength reduced to Cadre Strength and attached to D.A.C.	N⁰ 71026 Bomb. J.E. O'CONNELL. T.G.C. to H.Q. for repatriation.
			(Auth: I.O. R.D.A. N⁰ 12/1553 dated 29/1/19)	

January 31st 1919

E. Whitbread Capt RA
O.C 1/1st T.M.B. R.A.

Army Form C. 2118

WAR DIARY
or
INTELLIGENCE SUMMARY

of 218 F.M. 125 R.A.

(Erase heading not required.)

Instructions regarding War Diaries and Intelligence Summaries are contained in F.S. Regs., Part II. and the Staff Manual respectively. Title Pages will be prepared in manuscript.

Place	Date	Hour	Summary of Events and Information	Remarks and references to Appendices
Rollecourt	1.9.16		Training at Rollecourt.	
do.	2.9.16		do.	
do.	3.9.16		do. 2nd Lt. Innearity left for England on Special leave to get married.	
do.	4.9.16		do. Cpl. Redfern left for England on Special Leave for business.	
do.	5.9.16		All Medium Batteries moved to 5th Army area near Albert (cancelled) renamed at Rollecourt.	
do.	6.9.16		Resting at Rollecourt. Tried Williams' Bed for the first time. A success.	
do.	7.9.16		Still resting at Rollecourt.	
do.	8.9.16		do. do. do.	
Albert	9.9.16		The Battery moved into 5th Army area billetting at Albert.	
do.	10.9.16		Resting at Albert.	
do.	11.9.16		do. Dr. Biling evacuated sick.	
do.	12.9.16		Personnel of Battery went up to the line to help "A" & "B" Batteries 83rd Bde. to build advance gun pits.	
do.	13.9.16		Still building for "A" & "B" Batteries 83rd Bde.	
do.	14.9.16		Still building for "A" 83rd Bde. Capt. Bowen expressed a good opinion of the men's work.	

WAR DIARY
or
INTELLIGENCE SUMMARY

Army Form C. 2118

Place	Date	Hour	Summary of Events and Information	Remarks and references to Appendices
Albert	15.9.16		Resting at Albert.	
do.	16.9.16		do.	
do.	17.9.16		do. Had Church Parade and H.C. after. D.A.C. Chaplain	
do.	18.9.16		Battery again helping "A" 83rd Bde. to build fresh gun pits. Very wet.	
do.	19.9.16		do. do. do. do. Officers and few men went to Courcelette	
do.	20.9.16		Battery again helping "A" 83rd Bde. to build fresh gun pits. Finer weather.	
do.	21.9.16		Resting at Albert.	
do.	22.9.16		do. do. Good weather starts again.	
do.	23.9.16		Doing fatigues for 84th Bde. at Contalmaison.	
do.	24.9.16		do. do. do. do.	
do.	25.9.16		do. do. do. do.	
do.	26.9.16		Training at Albert.	
do.	27.9.16		do. do.	
do.	28.9.16		do. do.	
do.	29.9.16		do. do.	
do.	30.9.16		do. do.	

War Diary
for
October 1916

Z. 18th Dn. Trench.
Mortars

vol 4

Brigade Major
18th Divisional Artillery

> D.T.M.O.,
> 18th DIVISION.
> No. TMO120
> Date.

Forwarded herewith are War Diaries for X/18, and Z/18 T.M. Batteries, for the month of October.

Owing to OC Y/18 being wounded late in the month and there not being another officer with Y/18 the War Diary for that battery has not been compiled.

2/11/16

D. Bulter Capt.
D.T.M.O. 18th Div.

18th T.M. Batteries
(V, X, Y & Z)

WAR DIARY or INTELLIGENCE SUMMARY

Army Form C. 2118.

(Erase heading not required.)

Place	Date	Hour	Summary of Events and Information	Remarks and references to Appendices
Albert Aluicamps	Apl 30th	0.11"	French Mortar Batteries under my command were ordered to report to C.R.A V Corps. On arrival guides were provided by 2nd DTMO to show Battery Commanders the line. Batteries moved into action that night. V Corps now went to concentrate efforts to get one gun per battery into action and open fire while remainder of guns were being dug in. This policy was carried out and in consequence heavy casualties were suffered and work was delayed in the other portions. Full orders were two from "The Point to John Copse" which in addition to our front line & support line were in this sector.	
	May 1st		We were transferred to the 13th Corps. Altho this line that B guns in action in very bad positions & reported to BQ RA 13th Corps that it was extremely dangerous to fire from these positions, leaving they were reported by the Roche and obtained permission to cease fire for two days to enable B.C.'s to improve their positions. After this respite we again opened fire. We suffered very	

WAR DIARY or INTELLIGENCE SUMMARY

Army Form C. 2118.

(Erase heading not required.)

Place	Date	Hour	Summary of Events and Information	Remarks and references to Appendices
	6/11/9[?]		badly from Hostile Artillery + Mortar fire. On the arrival of the 31st D.A. we then had Artillery support and a Programme of fires was drawn up. By this time all our positions were repeated by the Arabs and on our firing, immediate retaliation took place in the form of 5.9 and gas-shells. An ammunition recess containing 59 rounds was hit by 5.9 + the whole exploded, throwing up the gun + causing B casualties. From now on, each Battery had guns put [out of] action in turn and I was exceedingly difficult to keep guns in action. On two occasions gun pits had to be abandoned owing to the devastating fire of enemy artillery. Two R.C's - one wounded, one suffering from shell-shock, followed the next day by another officer suffering from shell-shock. Men and N.C.O.'s began to go	

Army Form C. 2118.

WAR DIARY
or
INTELLIGENCE SUMMARY.
(Erase heading not required.)

Place	Date	Hour	Summary of Events and Information	Remarks and references to Appendices
			sick and were admitted to Hospital with nervous breakdown and it became increasingly difficult to carry on. I explained the situation to the Bde Major 31" D.A. who arranged for our relief by 33" D.A. on Oct 28th. X battery has now been in the line from Oct 1 to Oct 28th. Y & Z batteries relieved each other every few days. I was only evacuated to carry on during the last 5 days by the extremely good behaviour and bravery shown by my Men. Duro N.C.O.s showed conspicuous gallantry and I have recommended them for the D.C.M.	

Shrubs bf-
18 Div T.M.O.

Army Form C. 2118

WAR DIARY
or
INTELLIGENCE SUMMARY
(Erase heading not required.)

Z/18 T.M.B.

Instructions regarding War Diaries and Intelligence Summaries are contained in F.S. Regs., Part II and the Staff Manual respectively. Title Pages will be prepared in manuscript.

Place	Date	Hour	Summary of Events and Information	Remarks and references to Appendices
Hebuterne Ledin A.D.	11.10.16	4 P.M.	Relieved Y/18 T.M.B. This evening. - Trenches very wet. -	
	12.10.16	—	Put 2 guns into action 6-10 a.m. -	
	13.10.16	10 A.M.	Quiet - enemy activity. Had us 2 guns knocked out of action. -	
	14.10.16	—	Very fatiguing west position all day.	
	15.10.16	—	Fired 29 rds. To bay. - enemy artillery - fairly active. -	
	16.10.16	—	Fired 91 rds. to bay. Cutting German front-line wire from K.23.b.6.0.-K.23.d.9.6. and stores from K.23.a.9.2.	
	17.10.16	—	" one gun out. - The wrangle trench gnd in Dent ST.-	
	18.10.16	—	T.M. guns were buried toon - night Klemens 10 & 11. - by Both 5.9? - digging them out all day	
	19.10.16 15 noon	—	Fired 120 rds. to day. - Cutting the German wire in the following places — K 23.b.6.0. (12 ft wide 60 ft deep) also at K 23.d.7.9. (12 ft wide x 60 ft. deep) - K 23.d.8.8. (10 ft wide 90 ft. deep) " " " 20 " wide.) K 23 d.8.5. (20 ft wide 120 ft deep).	
	20.10.16	9AM & 5PM	Fired 69 rds.	
	21.10.16	5 PM	Came out of action. relieved by Y. B4y.	
	22.10.16	—	B4y at rest in Colincamps. (6 miles behind the line)	
	23.10.16	6 P.M.	Relieved Y/18 T.M.B4y this evening. - weather very wet.	
	24.10.16 10 & 2 AM			
	25.10.16	—	Fired 14 rds. Cutting German wire 50 yds south of Point 60 enemy artillery active	
			Shelled in heavily all a.m. - had gun in wrangle trench buried at 2.14. another at 7 a.m. 25th inst.- Sides of the gun-pits in Dent.S.T. as I slipping - had the night.	
	26.10.16	—	Fired 20 rds. - cutting German wire - 100 yds south of Point-60 - enemy. active. -	
	27.10.16	—	" 20 gun tank this evening. (also the railway bank)	
			Infantry - wiring. -	
	28.10.16	5 PM	Came out of action. -	
	29.10.16	—	At rest in Colincamp. - Joined at Beauvels + units undertaking to its men. -	
	30.10.16	—	Cleaning guns and stores in a.m. - fatigues in afternoon	
	31.10.16	—	" " polish the men at 6 this evening	

— J. D. Imeraity 2/Lt. 2. I F. T.M. B.

War Diary
for
November 1916

Z.1/18 M.T.M.Bty

Army Form C. 2118

WAR DIARY
or
INTELLIGENCE SUMMARY

(Erase heading not required.)

Instructions regarding War Diaries and Intelligence Summaries are contained in F. S. Regs., Part II. and the Staff Manual respectively. Title Pages will be prepared in manuscript.

Place	Date	Hour	Summary of Events and Information	Remarks and references to Appendices
COIGNEUX S.	1.11.16		Bathing at rest in Colincamp. Cleaning of guns & lines in A.M. & fatigues in the P.M.	
"	2.11.16	10 a.m.	Bath used in the men by stitching gun crews between stables. 2 P.M. smoke helmet inspection.	
"	3.11.16	9 a.m.	Parade inspection of clothes & field dressings. Paid the men at 6 P.M.	
"	4.11.16	9 a.m.	Inspection of gun ration.	
"	5.11.16	9 a.m.	Cleaning all guns & stores. 2 P.M. Issued winter under clothing.	
"	6.11.16	9 a.m.	Inspection of Bandoliers, & revolvers.	
"	7.11.16	2 P.M.	Issued gun cools, and mittens to the men.	
"	8.11.16	11 a.m.	Bath.	
"	9.11.16	9 a.m.	Cleaning guns, lines, & Lewis.	
"	10.11.16	9 a.m.	Inspection of all gun stores.	
"	11.11.16	9 a.m.	Parade. Physical Drill.	
"	12.11.16	6 P.M.	Paid the men out.	
"	13.11.16	—	Fatigues around camp.	
"	14.11.16	5:30 P.M.	Parade. Party of 30 men to R.E. Dump. Valentine to arrive. 19 O.R. — Truck winters returned to British camp 2 A.M.	

Army Form C. 2118.

WAR DIARY
or
INTELLIGENCE SUMMARY
(Erase heading not required.)

Instructions regarding War Diaries and Intelligence Summaries are contained in F. S. Regs., Part II. and the Staff Manual respectively. Title Pages will be prepared in manuscript.

Place	Date	Hour	Summary of Events and Information	Remarks and references to Appendices
COURCELMAISON	15.11.16	9 a.m.	Inspection of Field Telephones & stores - 2 P.M. packing of all stores. etc.	
"	16.11.16	10 a.m.	Left Courcelmaison by motor lorries via Battery; arrived at Albert 2. P.M. - good billets in the men.	
"	17.11.16	8. a.m.	Battery in Fatigues - cutting hardwood for R.E.s returned to Albert. 4. P.M.	
"	18.11.16	8.30 a.m.	" " Fatigues " " " " in R.E.s returned to Albert. 4. P.M. 4.30 Parade Sgt. Keene awarded Military Medal.	
"	19.11.16	1.30 P.M.	Sgt. Keene & Cpl. Freeday reps. allowed to attend Course of Instruction at 5th Army School of Instruction.—	
"	20.11.16	8.30 am	Fatigues for R.E.s—	
"	21.11.16	10.30 "	Bath in men in Albert & a clean change of underclothes—	
"	22.11.16	8.30 "	Fatigues for R.E. cutting hardwood	
"	23.11.16	8.30 "	" " " " " — 3.P.M. cleaning of guns.	
"	24.11.16	8.30 "	" " cutting hardwood	
"	25.11.16	—	" " Cpl Freeday went on leave	

Army Form C. 2118.

WAR DIARY
or
INTELLIGENCE SUMMARY
(Erase heading not required.)

Place	Date	Hour	Summary of Events and Information	Remarks and references to Appendices
26.11.16 allice	26.11.16	8.30 a.m.	Fatigue men for R.E.s	
	27.11.16	8.30	" "	
	28.11.16	8.30	" "	
	29.11.16	9.30	Parade. cleaning all guns – 4 new men joined from 1/8	
	30.11.16	9.30	Parade. – cleaning Rifles –	

J.D. Inverarity Lt.
O.C. Z.18. Trench Mortar Battery.
18th Division.

Confidential
War Diary of
"L.18 Trench Mortar Battery

From December 1st 1916   to December 31st 1916.
(Volume VI)

Army Form C. 2118.

WAR DIARY
or
INTELLIGENCE SUMMARY.
(Erase heading not required.)

Instructions regarding War Diaries and Intelligence Summaries are contained in F.S. Regs., Part II. and the Staff Manual respectively. Title pages will be prepared in manuscript.

Place	Date	Hour	Summary of Events and Information	Remarks and references to Appendices
Albert	1.12.16	8 a.m.	Parade. Inspection of anti-gas helmets. —	
"	2.12.16	8 "	Battery left Albert in 2 'buses at 9. a.m. Arrived at Petit Pont. 6. P.M. —	
Petit Pont	3.12.16	10 a.m.	Parade. cleaning all guns & limbers 2. P.M. Fatigues.	
"	4.12.16	9 "	S.T.M.O. Parade. 1.30. Bty. digging a working place for 82nd Bde. 2 mes. —	
"	6.12.16	9 "	Parade. rifle — drill. 2. P.M. anothe. drill: Inspection	
"	6.12.16	7.30 "	Physical drill. 9. a.m. Parade.	
"	7.12.16	9 "	Parade. cleaning up guns, anis & limbers. 2. P.M. gun drill.	
"	8.12.16	10 a.m.	gun drill. 2. P.M. rifle drill.	
"	9.12.16	10 "	" In inner of and. gunners.	
"	10.12.16	9 "	Parade. 11.30 a.m. church Parade. 2. P.M. foot & arm drill. —	
"	11.12.16	9 "	Parade & fired gun drill. 2. P.M. foot drill. Inspection drill. —	
"	12.12.16		cleaning guns & limbers. 10. a.m. revolver drill. In all N.C.O.s —	

WAR DIARY
or
INTELLIGENCE SUMMARY.

(Erase heading not required.)

Army Form C. 2118.

Place	Date	Hour	Summary of Events and Information	Remarks and references to Appendices
Celle Pd.	13.12.16	9 a.m.	Cleaning all guns. 10 a.m. Revolver Drill.	
"	14.12.16	9 "	Billets. 10 a.m. Revolver Drill. 2. P.M. Practise.	
"	15.12.16	8.45 "	Bty. on fatigues In 82nd Bde R.F.A. making a road.	
"	16.12.16	8.45 "	Bty. on " " " 2. P.M. revolver practise.	
"	17.12.16		fatigues In 82nd Bde. revolver practise in P.M.	
"	18.12.16	10.30	Ch. Ch. Parade. & officer in P.M. Medium T.M. Bn. r.s. Leaves.	
"	19.12.16	10 am	9 mm. running of the feris.	
"	20.12.16	8.45 "	Bty. on fatigues In 82nd Bde.	
"	21.12.16	8.45 "	" " " " 2. P.M. marching & saluting	
"	22.12.16	8.45	Drill under Sgr. Maj. of 82nd Bde.	
"	23.12.16	10 am	Parade. and Pay. n. Inoculation In Bty. In the Temple. Silence.	

WAR DIARY
INTELLIGENCE SUMMARY

Army Form C. 2118.

Place	Date	Hour	Summary of Events and Information	Remarks and references to Appendices
Oxtel Out	24/12/16	8.4'6'	Bly on Fatigues In 82nd Bde. R.F.A.	
"	25/12/16	9.a.m	Church Parade. 7. P.M. Christmas Dinner In the Battery.	
"	26.12.16		Battery Fatigues	
"	27/12/16		Do.	
"	28/12/16		Battery supplied fort to go to 61st Do/b staying at Abville for a night	
"	29/12/16		Battery move to Abville arriving the same day. The J.S Waggons were waiting there were loaded and despatched the remainder of stores and Battery personnel stayed at Abbeville for the night	
"	30/12/16		Battery Personnel and stores moved to 61st Do/b	
"	31/12/16		Battery Fatigues and also 5 men from 61st Bde. 6. A" Dr.	

J. D. Invanity Lt.
OC. Z. 18. T.M. Bly.

Army Form C. 2118.

WAR DIARY
or
INTELLIGENCE SUMMARY.
(Erase heading not required.)

Instructions regarding War Diaries and Intelligence Summaries are contained in F. S. Regs., Part II. and the Staff Manual respectively. Title pages will be prepared in manuscript.

Place	Date	Hour	Summary of Events and Information	Remarks and references to Appendices
Bouzincourt	1/1/17	8.45 a.m	All available men for fatigues building Huts & drawing Material	18 Div H⁺ Qrs
	2		" " " " " " " "	" "
	3		" " " " " " " "	" "
	4		" " " " " " " "	" "
	5		" " " " " " " "	" "
	6		" " " " " " " "	" "
	7		" " " " " " " "	" "
	8		" " " " " " " "	" "
	9		" " " " " " " "	" "
	10		" " " " " " " "	" "
	11		" " " " " " " "	" "
	12		" " " " " " " "	" "
	13		Battery Personel left Bouzincourt at 11:30 for Authuille Wood. Arrived at 2ᵖᵐ	
Authuille Wood	14	8.15 a.m	The rest of the Day was spent in erecting Tents for Officers & Men.	
			13 Men on fatigue for 84ᵗʰ Bde R.F.A.	
	15		11 Men " " " " "	
	16		" " 2 Men on fatigues for M.O. 82ⁿᵈ Bde R.F.A.	
	17		" " " " " "	
	18	8.30 a m	" " " " " "	
	19		" " " " " "	
	20		" " " " " "	
	21		7 Men " " " 3 " " 8 & 2ⁿᵈ Bde R.F.A. & Battʸ fg out at 6 ᵖᵐ R.F.A.	

Army Form C. 2118.

WAR DIARY
or
INTELLIGENCE SUMMARY.
(Erase heading not required.)

Instructions regarding War Diaries and Intelligence Summaries are contained in F.S. Regs., Part II. and the Staff Manual respectively. Title pages will be prepared in manuscript.

Place	Date	Hour	Summary of Events and Information	Remarks and references to Appendices
Aultin the Wood	22nd	8 30	7 Men on Fatigues for R.F.A. 2 & 4 Men to M.O. & 2nd Bde. R.F.A.	
	23rd	"	All available Men on fatigues for 82nd Bde. R.F.A.	
	24	"	" " " " " "	
	25	"	" " " " " "	
	26	"	" " " " " "	
	27	"	" " " " " "	
	28	"	" " " " " "	
	29	"	All available Men on fatigues for D/82nd R.F.A.	
	30	"	" " " " " "	
	31	"	" " " " " "	

J.D. Inverarity Lt.
O.C. T.M.B.
-8-2-18

Army Form C. 2118.

WAR DIARY
or
INTELLIGENCE SUMMARY.
(Erase heading not required.)

Instructions regarding War Diaries and Intelligence Summaries are contained in F.S. Regs., Part II. and the Staff Manual respectively. Title pages will be prepared in manuscript.

Place	Date	Hour	Summary of Events and Information	Remarks and references to Appendices
In the field	1/2/17		All available men for 2/84 on Fatigue. Rifle & Revolver inspection 4.30 pm	
	2/2/17		" " " "	
	3/2/17		" " " "	
	4/2/17		" " " "	
	5/2/17		" " " "	
	6/2/17		" " " "	
	7/2/17		" " " "	
	8/2/17		" " " "	
	9/2/17		" " " "	
	10/2/17		6 Men for Fatigue 83 Bde R.F.A. 6 men on fatigue for 15 Div. D.A.C.	
	11/2/17		10 " " " A/82 R.F.A	
	12/2/17		10 " " " B/82 "	
	13/2/17		10 " " " " "	
	14/2/17		" " " " "	
	15/2/17		All available removing ammunition for 83 & 84th Bde R.F.A.	
	16/2/17		" " " " "	
	17/2/17		" " " " "	
	18/2/17		10 men on fatigue for A/82 R.F.A.	
	19/2/17		" " " 84 Bde. R.F.A. H.Q.rs	

N. Wood Lieut.
N.B. Off.
O.C. 1/18 T.M.B. 82nd R.F.A

Army Form C. 2118.

WAR DIARY
or
INTELLIGENCE SUMMARY.
(Erase heading not required.)

Instructions regarding War Diaries and Intelligence Summaries are contained in F. S. Regs., Part II. and the Staff Manual respectively. Title pages will be prepared in manuscript.

Place	Date	Hour	Summary of Events and Information	Remarks and references to Appendices
Anthuille Wood	20/2/17		All available men & N.C.O on Fatigue from 8 2" Bde R.F.A.	
	21/2/17		" "	
	22/2/17		" "	
	23/2/17		" "	
	24/2/17		Busy stand by for orders	
	25/2/17		All available men & N.C.O on Fatigue from Det 6 1/2 Divisional ammunition Dump	
	26/2/17		" "	
	27/2/17		" "	
	28/2/17		" "	

Z 18T-M.B.

Army Form C. 2118.

WAR DIARY
or
INTELLIGENCE SUMMARY.
(Erase heading not required.)

Instructions regarding War Diaries and Intelligence Summaries are contained in F.S. Regs., Part II. and the Staff Manual respectively. Title pages will be prepared in manuscript.

Place	Date	Hour	Summary of Events and Information	Remarks and references to Appendices
Australia Wood	1/3/17		All Available Men on Ammunition Fatigue for 18th D.A.B.	
	2/3/17		" " " " " " " "	
	3/3/17		" " " " " " " "	
	4/3/17		" " " " " " " "	
	5/3/17		" " " " " " " "	
	6/3/17		" " " " " " " "	
	7/3/17		" " " " " " " "	
	8/3/17		" " " " " " " "	
	9/3/17		" " " " " " " "	
	10/3/17		" " " " " " " "	
	11/3/17		The whole Battery turned round & began into camp	
	12/3/17		all Available men on Fatigue from 18th D.A.B	
	13/3/17		" " " " " " " "	
	14/3/17		" " " " " " " "	
	15/3/17		" " " " " " " "	
	16/3/17		" " " " " " " "	
	17/3/17		" " " " " " " "	
	18/3/17		" " " " " " " "	
	19/3/17		About 6 o'ct an advance of 2 div D.A.C. 18 div at Australia passage	
	20/3/17		D.A.C. the remainder clearing up camp	
	21/3/17		8 men on Fatigues for No 2 Sec	
Aveluy Village	22/3/17			
	23/3/17			

Army Form C. 2118.

WAR DIARY
or
INTELLIGENCE SUMMARY.
(Erase heading not required.)

Instructions regarding War Diaries and Intelligence Summaries are contained in F. S. Regs., Part II. and the Staff Manual respectively. Title pages will be prepared in manuscript.

Place	Date	Hour	Summary of Events and Information	Remarks and references to Appendices
Christchurch NZ	24/3/17	8 am	Men on fatigue for No 2 sec D.A.C. & Div	
	25/3/17		Struck camp and moved to Awapuni Station & entrained	
	26/3/17	6.30 am	Left Awapuni at 3.30 am and detrained at Palmerston at 6.30 am. Entrained and proceeded to Bulls Gate at 8 am	
	27/3/17	7.30	Detrained at Bulls Gate at 7.30. All Battery Personnel slept in Y.M.C.A.	
	28/3/17		Entrained for Hazelhurst at 5 pm arrived about 6 am. Battery personnel marched to Billets	
	29/3/17		All guns & stores moved from station to Billets & the remainder at the day cleaning Equipment	
	30/3/17	10.30 am	Inspection of Ammunition & Rifles. 11.30 am Inspection of Equipment & kit. Gun Drill at 1 pm. Cleaning guns & Billets	
	31/3/17		Battery cleaning Guns & Stores	

J. D. Inverarity Lt.
OC. Z.18. T.M.B.

War Diary
for
April. 1917

Trench Mortar
Batteries

V/18
X/18
Y/18
Z/18

Confidential

Headquarters
18th Divl. Artillery   No 674

Herewith war diaries
for month of April for
the Batteries under my
command, please

1/5/17   D Butler Capt
         D Mo 18 Div

D.T.M.Bty
Vol 10

War Diary
for
April. 1917

18th Divisional Artillery

~~82nd Brigade R.F.A~~
~~83rd Brigade R.F.A~~
~~18th Div. Amm. Col.~~
~~V/18 H.T.M. Battery~~
~~X/18 M.T.M. Battery~~
~~Y/18 M.T.M. Battery~~
~~Z/18 M.T.M. Battery~~

Army Form C. 2118.

WAR DIARY
or
INTELLIGENCE SUMMARY.
(Erase heading not required.)

Place	Date	Hour	Summary of Events and Information	Remarks and references to Appendices
Highland	1/4/17	—		
	2/4/17	10 a.m	2.30 p.m Marching Drill	
	3/4/17	10 a.m	" "	
	3/4/17	10 a.m	" "	
	4/4/17	10 a.m	5.30 p.m Pay out	
	5/4/17	10 a.m	2.30 p.m Marching Drill	
	6/4/17	10 a.m	" Rifle Drill	
	7/4/17	10 a.m	2 p.m Marching Drill	
	8/4/17	10 a.m	2 p.m Revolver Drill	
	9/4/17	10 a.m	2 p.m Marching Drill	
	10/4/17	10 a.m	3 p.m Football Match Medium v R.A.H.Q 2nd	
	11/4/17	10 a.m	2 p.m Marching Drill	
	12/4/17	10 a.m	2 p.m "	
	13/4/17	10 a.m	2 p.m "	
	14/4/17	10 a.m	2 p.m Smoke Helmet Inspection	
	15/4/17	10 a.m	2 p.m Rifle Drill	
	16/4/17	10 a.m	2 p.m "	
	17/4/17	10 a.m	2 p.m Revolver Drill	

Army Form C. 2118.

WAR DIARY
or
INTELLIGENCE SUMMARY.
(Erase heading not required.)

Instructions regarding War Diaries and Intelligence Summaries are contained in F. S. Regs., Part II. and the Staff Manual respectively. Title pages will be prepared in manuscript.

Place	Date	Hour	Summary of Events and Information	Remarks and references to Appendices
Anglesqueville	19/4/17	10 a.m	Gun Drill	
	20/4/17	10 a.m	"	
	21/4/17	10 a.m	R.A. Church Parade	
	22/4/17	10 a.m	Gun Drill	
	23/4/17	10 a.m	Gun Drill	
	24/4/17	10 a.m		
		2 p.m	Marching Drill	
		2 p.m	"	
		2 p.m	Inspection of Breech Action	
		2 p.m	Rifle Drill	
		5 p.m	bag out	
	25/4/17	7 a.m	Loading trains for 18th D.A.C.B. Battery Convoyed left HAZEBROUCK at 5.30 p.m
			arrived at OBLINGHEIM at 7.30 p.m	
Oblingheim	26/4/17	10 a.m	Cleaning Guns & Stores	
	27/4/17		Battery left OBLINGHEIM at 6 p.m arrived at Heuchin 8.30 p.m	
Heuchin	28/4/17	10 a.m	Cleaning Guns & Stores	
	29/4/17		Sunday	
	30/4/17	8 a.m	Battery left HEUCHIN arrived at WAILLY 2.30 p.m arrived at BEAURAINES

Jo Guinlothy — Lt
O.C. I/18 T.M.B.

Vol XI

War Diaries
for
MAY. 1917

18th T.M. Batteries:-
V/18
X/18
Y/18
Z/18

Imo/59.

Headquarters
18th Divisional Artillery

Attached please find War Diaries for May 1917 for the Batteries under my Command.

3/6/17   A Butler Capt
         D Imo 18th Div

Army Form C. 2118.

WAR DIARY
or
INTELLIGENCE SUMMARY.
(Erase heading not required.)

Instructions regarding War Diaries and Intelligence Summaries are contained in F. S. Regs., Part II. and the Staff Manual respectively. Title pages will be prepared in manuscript.

Place	Date	Hour	Summary of Events and Information	Remarks and references to Appendices
Beaucamps	1/5/17	9.30 am	Gun Drill and Cleaning Stores	
	2/5/17	9 am	Inspection of rifles & revolvers	
	3/5/17	10 am	Inspection of Smoke Helmets & Box respirators 2 p.m Inspection of Mess Tins	
	4/5/17	10 am	Cleaning Guns & Stores	
	5/5/17	11 am	Rifle & Revolver Drill	
	6/5/17	9 am	Gun Drill	
	7/5/17	9.30	Rifle & Revolver Inspection	
	8/5/17	9.30	Physical Drill & Battery Fatigues	
	9/5/17	9 am	Gun Drill & Inspection of Equipment	
	10/5/17	9.30	Cleaning Gun & Stores	
	11/5/17	9.30	Inspection of Smoke Helmets & Box Respirators	
	12/5/17	9.30	Inspection of Guns & Battery Personnel By G.O.C.R.A. 18th Div	
	13/5/17	9.30	Gun Drill & Signalling	
	14/5/17	9.30	Battery Fatigues	
	15/5/17	9.30	Inspection of Rifles & Revolvers & Drill	
	16/5/17	7.30	Physical Drill & Gun Drill	
	17/5/17	9 am	Battery Fatigues & Physical Drill & Inspection	
	18/5/17	9.30	"	
	19/5/17	9.30	"	

Army Form C. 2118.

WAR DIARY
or
INTELLIGENCE SUMMARY.

(Erase heading not required.)

Place	Date	Hour	Summary of Events and Information	Remarks and references to Appendices
Amiens	20/5/17		Battery Fatigues, Drills & Inspection	
	21/5/17		"	
	22/5/17		"	
	23/5/17		"	
	24/5/17		"	
	25/5/17		All Battery Personnel attached to R.A. 16 Div for Instruction	
	26/5/17		"	
	27/5/17		"	
	28/5/17		"	
	29/5/17		"	
	30/5/17		"	
	31/5/17		"	

Jo. Inverarity - Lt
O C Z/18. T.M.B. R.A.

18th D.T.M.Btys

V/18
X/18
Y/18
Z/18

June. 1917

Army Form C. 2118

WAR DIARY
or
INTELLIGENCE SUMMARY.
(Erase heading not required.)

Instructions regarding War Diaries and Intelligence Summaries are contained in F. S. Regs., Part II. and the Staff Manual respectively. Title pages will be prepared in manuscript.

Place	Date	Hour	Summary of Events and Information	Remarks and references to Appendices
In the Field	1/6/17		Battery Personnel on Fatigues for 18th Divl Artillery.	
	2/1/17		Battery Stores removed by G.S. Wagons supplied by the D.A.C. from Bavincourt to Henu.	
	3/6/17		18 men on Fatigue for 18th Divl Artillery	
	4/6/17		" " " " "	
	5/6/17		" " " " "	
	6/6/17		" " " " "	
	7/6/17		" " " " "	
	8/6/17		" " " " "	
	9/6/17		" " " " "	
	10/6/17		" " " " "	
	11/6/17		" " " " "	
	12/6/17		" " " " "	
	13/6/17		" " " " "	
	14/6/17		All men returned from Divl Fatigues to be rearranged between Batteries	
	15/6/17		Smoke Helmet. Gas Ration & Equipment Inspections.	
	16/6/17		9 men on Fatigues for A/82 & 4 men on Fatigues B/82	
	17/6/17		" " " " " " " " "	
	18/6/17		" " " " " " " " "	
	19/6/17		" " " " " " " " "	
	20/6/17		" " " " " " " " "	

Army Form C. 2118.

WAR DIARY
or
INTELLIGENCE SUMMARY.
(Erase heading not required.)

Instructions regarding War Diaries and Intelligence Summaries are contained in F. S. Regs., Part II. and the Staff Manual respectively. Title pages will be prepared in manuscript.

Place	Date	Hour	Summary of Events and Information	Remarks and references to Appendices
In the Field	21/4/17		All Battery Personnel returned from to Unit from 18 Div Artillery	
	22/4/17		Battery Fatigues. Drill & Inspections	
	23/4/17		"	
	24/4/17		"	
	25/4/17		"	
	26/4/17		"	
	27/4/17		Battery Personnel & store removed from at 10 am and arrived at Div rest camp about 2 pm	
	28/4/17		6 men on Fatigue at the Div shallop sports ground. The remainder on Camp Fatigues	
	29/4/17		6 men on Fatigue at the " " "	
	30/4/17		8 " " " " "	

for O.C. 27/18 T.M.B

Headquarters Confidential
18th Divl Artillery
                    D/mo814.

Herewith War Diaries for the Batteries under my Command for the Month of June 1917

Would you kindly acknowledge receipt.

7/7/17 D Butler Capt
                    D/mo 18 Dn

War Diary
for
July 1917

18th T.M.G Batteries:
V/18
X/18
Y/18
Z/18

Confidential

To/
Headquarters   Jno 899
18th Divl Artillery

Please find
attached, War Diaries
for the Batteries under
my Command for the
Month of July 1917

3/8/17   A Butter Capt
                D/no 18 Div

Army Form C. 2118.

WAR DIARY
or
INTELLIGENCE SUMMARY
(Erase heading not required.)

Instructions regarding War Diaries and Intelligence Summaries are contained in F.S. Regs., Part II. and the Staff Manual respectively. Title pages will be prepared in manuscript.

Place	Date	Hour	Summary of Events and Information	Remarks and references to Appendices
In field	1/7/17		6 men on fatigues for Div Hqrs. Remainder fatigues and Nivel.	
	2/7/17		Battery Fatigues. Remainder of day attending 15th Div. sports.	
	3/7/17		" moved by Lorry from Nivelles rest area to Woellens	
	4/7/17		" arrived at Woellens & relieved at Goodrich at 11.30 P.M.	
	5/7/17		Bty. marched to Reels inside Stienvoorde at 10 P.M. & bivouacked by Lorry from station	
	6/7/17		Bty. fatigues. Inspection of Motors. Kennels & gun cleaning.	
	7/7/17		" " " "	
		6 P.M.	Motor Coach & jacketed guns & Lines. 8.30 A.M. Lorries	
		arrived.	Bty. personnel & lines left Steenvoorde at 9 A.M.	
			arrived at Dickebusch at 1 P.M. 3 P.M. Cleaning	
	12/7/17		guns & lines.	
			Bty. fatigues & Nivel.	
	13/7/17	9 A.M.	Inspection of Motors Kennels	
	14/7/17		received orders to go into action. Left DICKYBUSCH @ 6.30 P.M. Bty. in 2 G.S. wagons – personnel marched Corner, Hell Fire Corner. arrived ZILLEBEKE at 9.30 P.M.	

A 5834 Wt. W 4973/M 682 750,000 8/16 D.D. & L. Ltd. Forms/C.2113/13.

Army Form C. 2118.

WAR DIARY
or
INTELLIGENCE SUMMARY.
(Erase heading not required.)

Place	Date	Hour	Summary of Events and Information	Remarks and references to Appendices
14.7.17 ZILLEBEKE.	14/7/17 cont'd	9.50 P.M	Received message from Australians to stay at ZILLEBEKE SIDINGS in view of enemy was about to let up his supply barrage.	
	15/7/17	6.30 a.m.	100th O.R. gun. position from Australians. 1 Neg. rds in crate. Crawl. Tunnel. for 2 officers 1 20 men. In P.M. OBSy of Building. Gun Pits. at I.24.d.5.0.85 & I.24.c.5.0.85 + I.24.c.65.80 - Ry HOOGE. M.A.P. I.24.d.36.22. + Position near 70.000 - Bty busy building Gun Pits.	
	16/7/17		Registered the Bty Ts. Nay. - fired 12 rounds. - The Ted of No.1. gun shots in Rally.	
	17/7/17		Fired 31 rounds to Nay. 2 snipers cul-gaps in enemy wire at - J.19.a.45.80 and I.24 & 95.75. -	
	18/7/17		Fired 26 rounds to Nay. cul-gaps in enemy wire at T.19.a.10.65 T.19.a.50.00 enemy retaliated heavily in our front line.	
	19/7/17		Fired 49 rounds to day & 2 needs. - cul-gaps in enemy wire at - T.19.a.10.55 T.19.a.10.50 T.19.a.30.20	

Army Form C. 2118.

WAR DIARY
or
INTELLIGENCE SUMMARY.
(Erase heading not required.)

Instructions regarding War Diaries and Intelligence Summaries are contained in F. S. Regs., Part II. and the Staff Manual respectively. Title pages will be prepared in manuscript.

Place	Date	Hour	Summary of Events and Information	Remarks and references to Appendices
ZILLEBEKE.	19/7/17	cont.	Blew in enemy trench 100 yds. S. of J.24.b.95.80 wheels of a car of some oil were observed to be thrown into the air. fired up. 1.3.4 Gun No. 2 - Position not ready yet. Enemy did not retaliate	
	20/7/17		Fired 10 rds. this evening - fired in enemy trench gun emplacement on account of some in enemy machine gun emplacement at I. t. 80.90. smoke in the ... fire on account of BEDFORDS reporting to be relief of BEDFORDS. enemy Vickers observation very good. Enemy a. Meeny active all day. Fired 64 rounds this morning. 4 cal. gaps in enemy wire at T. a. 10.60 / T. a. 10.55 / T. a. 30.25 / T. a. 30.22 Fired 20 rounds on W. O. T. a. 10.60. no wire war. L. to	
	21/7/14		cut in the ground behind. seen from the O.P. but a quantity of wire was ob- served to there ef at every round. Fired on enemy Bay trench at T. a. 10.45 on 3rd round a large quantity of white smoke was observed to rise from the top. Enemy Battery very active	

WAR DIARY or INTELLIGENCE SUMMARY

Army Form C. 2118.

Place	Date	Hour	Summary of Events and Information	Remarks and references to Appendices
ZILLEBEKE	21/7/17	a.m.	all. nav. This afternoon an enemy aeroplane dropped a flare over 3 & 4 guns at It 40.15-20" afterwards 1 enemy shell fell 20 yds. over.	
			- Fired 78 rds. - Cw. gaps in enemy-wire at- T. 19 a. 45. 90 T. 19 a. 43. 09 T. 19 a. 15. 35 T. 19 c. 40. 65 T. 19 a. 09. 53	
	22/7		Fired 5" rounds nil. Trench al- T. 19a. 09. 45. when just en. el. appeared to have been driven off. During the night - enemy artillery very active between 2 and 5 this afternoon. was active ti fire burst rounds fired as N. T 9m of Bou t. Causing it to explode in muzzle of tuncher - Inflicting Tenifer silencer gun in retirement - was euru fire.	
	23/7/7		. Fired. 23 rds. Cw. gaps in enemy wire at- I.24 L.95.80 and T.19a.10.43 - Sub.3.4 Position.	
	24/7/7		Hour in - Fired 20 rds Cw gap in wire al- I.24 R.95.80 and T.19 a 05'.29. -	
			Michelment's rebuilding this ell -	

WAR DIARY
or
INTELLIGENCE SUMMARY.
(Erase heading not required.)

Army Form C. 2118.

Place	Date	Hour	Summary of Events and Information	Remarks and references to Appendices
ZILLEBEKE	25/7/17		No fires allowed to be lit in Crab Crawl & nep. ceb. so are tot. meal. A ray too is to carried up to the men from ZILLEBEKE 3/4 of an hour each. Bty relieving Pits ad- noep.	
	26/7/17		" "	
	27/7/17		Fired 100 rounds. Cut gaps in enemy wire at T.19.a.10.50, T.19.a.10.40, I.24.B.95.90 and flew in Trenches at T.19.a.100.70, T.19.a.10.44, T.19.a.12.42, T.19.a.20.35, T.19.c.40.90, T.19.c.45.88. Enemy Artillery retaliated, firing in the self-section.	
	28/7/17		Fired 25 rds on M.G emplacement at T.19.a.80.85. Also diver Pits were observed. Also noep. JAM. TRENCH - from T.19.a.25.55 to T.19.a.55.50 - enemy retaliated heavily.	
	29/7/17		Fired 25 rounds into on JAM. TRENCH from T.19.a.25.55 to T.19.a.55.50. Also one Gun OP. flew in	

WAR DIARY
or
INTELLIGENCE SUMMARY

Army Form C. 2118.

Place	Date	Hour	Summary of Events and Information	Remarks and references to Appendices
ZILLEBEKE.	30.7.19	6.30 A.M.	Fired 40 rds. li. way.. Fired on Enemy Trench June T.19.a.10.45" to T.19.a.30.60". & M.G. emplacement at T.19.a.50.85". No. 3 gun thrown u/s during artillery action. Observation fair.	
		6.30 P.M.	Received news that T.M.O. li. will draw 3 by. carried guns to ZILLEBEKE. & loaded them onto G.S. wagon. — waited for June ZILLEBEKE to DICKYBUSCH. arrived 11. P.M. —	
	31/7/19 A.M.		— Men resting throughout the day. —	

Jn. Quneardy LT.
a. 7.16.
— T.M.B. —

Army Form C. 2118.

WAR DIARY
or
INTELLIGENCE SUMMARY.
(Erase heading not required.)

Instructions regarding War Diaries and Intelligence Summaries are contained in F. S. Regs., Part II. and the Staff Manual respectively. Title pages will be prepared in manuscript.

Place	Date	Hour	Summary of Events and Information	Remarks and references to Appendices
Bichy-Bual	1.8.17	9. a.m.	Parade. Cleaning Guns & Olio etc.	
	2.8.17	10 "	" Inspection of D'uoble Relnub, & Cleaning Guns.	
		2. P.M.	Rifle and revolver Inspection.	
	3.8.17	9. a.m.	Parade - Cleaning Guns & Olio - & Inspection of new intervo	
	4.8.17	9 "	" and Inspection of Gun. Olivo etc..	
	5.8.17	10 "	" Cleaning all Guns & Olio.	
	6.8.17	9 "	Fatiques.	
	7.9.17	9 "	Parade. Cleaning Olivo Guns.	
	8.8.17	10 "	Parade & revolver. nill..	
	9.8.17	10.30 "	" Jes Bathe. & Clean Change of underclothing.	
	10.8.17	9 "	" Inspection of D'uoble Helnub. 2.P.M. Inspection of gun & Olivo.	
	11.8.17	10 "	Parade & rifle & revolver. & nil.	
	12.8.17	9 & 2 P.h	Fatiques around - Camp. 1. P.M. Pay-ord. gt	
	13.8.17	10 "	" " " " 1. P.M. Pay-ord. gt.	
	14.8.17	10 "	Parade & disinfecting of D'iell, and Blankels. 6. men attached 15/62 or fatiques.	
	15.8.17	11 "	Kit - Inspection.	
	16.8.17	9 "	Parade. Gun. Cleaning.	
	17.8.17 "		Fatiques.	
	18. PM	"	Cleaning Guns & Olivo & Fatiques.	
	19.8.17	"	Parade & practicing Signalling.	
	20.8.17	"	Gun cleaning. 6.30 P.M. Inspection of Q works - Helnub.	
	21.8.17	"	" " " "	
	22.8.17	"	" " 6 " " of Revolvers & Rifles..	
	23.8.17		" " " of Revolvers & Rifles..	

Army Form C. 2118.

WAR DIARY
or
INTELLIGENCE SUMMARY.
(Erase heading not required.)

Instructions regarding War Diaries and Intelligence Summaries are contained in F. S. Regs., Part II. and the Staff Manual respectively. Title pages will be prepared in manuscript.

Place	Date	Hour	Summary of Events and Information	Remarks and references to Appendices
"	24/8/17	9 am	- Bhy on fatigues.	
"	25/8/17	"	" " "	
"	26/8/17	"	Cleaning - guns.	
"	27/8/17	"	" "	
"	28/8/17	"	" "	
"	29/8/17	"	5' am Reveille 6 am Breakfast. 7.15' Parade - Lyj. Sichy. Bud. D. B. a.h. on leave	
"	30/8/17	"	cursed - OUDEZEELE at 2.P.M. - putting up tents etc in O.M.	
"	31/8/17	9 "	Parade - cleaning guns & improving - Camp. etc.	

Jn. Menarily KT.
- 2-18 . T. M. B. —
- 31/8/17 —

WAR DIARY
INTELLIGENCE SUMMARY

(Erase heading not required.)

Army Form C. 2118

2/18 Dm Batt

Place	Date	Hour	Summary of Events and Information	Remarks and references to Appendices
OUDERZEELE	1.9.17	7.30	Marching Drill. 9.30 cleaning guns and stores.	
	2.9.17	"	Marching Drill. 9.30 smoke helmet Inspection. 2.P.M cleaning guns and stores.	
	3.9.17	"	Marching Drill. 9.30 Inspection of rifles and Revolvers.	
	4.9.17	"	Marching Drill. 9.30 cleaning guns and stores 2.P.M Inspection of Iron rations.	
	5.9.17	"	Marching Drill. 9.30 rifle and revolver practice. 2.PM cleaning guns.	
	6.9.17	"	Marching Drill. 9.30 rifle Drill. 2.P.M Inspection of smoke helmets.	
	7.9.17	"	Marching Drill. 9.30 Inspection of guns and stores 2.P.M Fatigues.	
	8.9.17	"	Marching Drill. 9.30 cleaning guns and stores.	
	9.9.17	"	Marching Drill. 9.30 rifle practice for all N.C.O's and men. 2.P.M cleaning guns.	
	10.9.17	"	Marching Drill. 9.30 cleaning guns and stores. 2.P.M. smoke helmet Inspection.	
	11.9.17	"	Marching Drill. 9.30 rifle and revolver practice. 2.P.M cleaning guns.	
	12.9.17	"	Marching Drill. 9.30 Inspection of guns and stores.	
	13.9.17	"	Marching Drill. 9.30 rifle practice. 2.P.M smoke helmet Drill.	
	14.9.17	"	Marching Drill. 9.30 cleaning guns and stores.	
	15.9.17	"	Marching Drill. 9.30 rifle practice. 2.P.M. Inspection of guns and stores.	
	16.9.17	"	Marching Drill. 9.30 gun cleaning. 2.P.M. Rifle practice.	
	17.9.17	"	Marching Drill. 9.20 Inspection of rifles and revolvers. 2.P.M Inspection smoke helmets.	
	18.9.17	"	Marching Drill. 9.30 cleaning guns and stores. 2.P.M Fatigues.	
	19.9.17	"	Marching Drill. 9.30 rifle practice for N.C.O's and men. 2.P.M. gun cleaning.	
	20.9.17	"	5am Reveille. 6.30 breakfast. 8.am Parade. left OUDERZEELE 9.am entrained arrived SEB DUES at 12.30. 2.pm putting up tents and improving camp.	
SEROUES	21.9.17	"	Marching Drill. 9.30 cleaning guns and stores. 2.P.M. smoke helmet Inspection.	
	22.9.17	"	Marching Drill. 9.30 rifle and revolver Inspection. 2.P.M Fatigued.	
	23.9.17	"	Marching Drill. 9.30 cleaning guns and stores.	
	24.9.17	"	5am Reveille. 6am Breakfast. 7.am left SEROUES arrived in ZEGGAR CAPPEL. 12.30.	

Army Form C. 2118

WAR DIARY
or
INTELLIGENCE SUMMARY
(Erase heading not required.)

Instructions regarding War Diaries and Intelligence Summaries are contained in F. S. Regs., Part II. and the Staff Manual respectively. Title Pages will be prepared in manuscript.

Place	Date	Hour	Summary of Events and Information	Remarks and references to Appendices
POPERINGHE	25-9-17		5 am Reveille. 6.30 Breakfast. 9.30 left ZEGGAR CAPPEL. arrived in POPERINGHE. 12.30. 2. PM putting up Tents and Improving Camp.	
	26-9-17	9.30	Marching Drill. 9.30 Inspection of Rifles and Revolvers. 2. PM Cleaning Guns.	
	27-9-17	"	Marching Drill. 9.30 Cleaning Guns and Stores. 2. PM Smoke helmet Inspection.	
	28-9-17	"	Marching Drill. 9.30 Cleaning Guns and Stores. 3. PM left POPERINGHE. arrived at VLMERTINGH 5.30. 6 PM Improving Camp.	
VLMERTINGH	29-9-17	"	Marching Drill. 9.30 Cleaning Guns and Stores. 2. PM Rifle Inspection.	
	30-9-17		5 am Reveille 6 am Parade 9 men attached to 291 Brigade. R.F.A for fatigues.	

J. Innerarity. Lieut.
I 18. T.M.B.

~~18TH DIVISIONAL ARTILLERY.~~

18TH DIVISION TRENCH MORTAR BATTERIES.

W A R   D I A R Y

- FOR -

MONTH OF OCTOBER, 1917.

Army Form C. 2118.

Z/18 T.M. Batty

Vol/6

WAR DIARY
or
INTELLIGENCE SUMMARY.
(Erase heading not required.)

Place	Date	Hour	Summary of Events and Information	Remarks and references to Appendices
VLAMERTINGHE	1-10-17		8 men attached to 291 Brigade R.F.A, 4 men attached to C.83 Brigade R.F.A,	
	2-10-17		do	
	3-10-17		do	
	4-10-17		do	
	5-10-17		do	
	6-10-17		do	
	7-10-17		do	
	8-10-17		do	
	9-10-17		8 men returned from 291 Brigade R.F.A, 4 men attached B. to C.83 Brigade R.F.A	
	10-10-17		6 men attached to ZOUAVE DUMP. A.M.R.P, 4 men returned from C.83 Brigade R.F.A	
	11-10-17		6 men attached to ZOUAVE DUMP. A.M.R.P	
	12-10-17		6 men attached to D.83 Brigade R.F.A, 7 men attached R.F.A	
CHATEAU	13-10-17		St VLAMERTINGHE 12.30 P.M. Arrived at CHATEAU TROIS TOURS 3.20 P.M.	
TROIS TOURS R.S.	14-10-17		6 men attached to ZOUAVE DUMP A.M.R.P, 7 men attached to D.83 Brigade R.F.A	
	15-10-17		do	
	16-10-17		do	
	17-10-17		do	
	18-10-17		do	
	19-10-17		6 men attached to ZOUAVE DUMP A.M.R.P, 7 men attached to D.83 Brigade, 2 men B.83 Brigade F. Ally	
	20-10-17		do	
	21-10-17		do	
	22-10-17		do	

Army Form C. 2118.

WAR DIARY
of
INTELLIGENCE SUMMARY.
(Erase heading not required.)

Instructions regarding War Diaries and Intelligence Summaries are contained in F. S. Regs., Part II. and the Staff Manual respectively. Title pages will be prepared in manuscript.

Place	Date	Hour	Summary of Events and Information	Remarks and references to Appendices
Chateau des Trois Tours	23.10.17		2 men attached to 2/0 V.A. Dum D.A.N.R. & 7 men attached to D.83 Brigade, 2 men D.V 2 Brigade	
	24.10.17		do	do
	25.10.17		6 men returned to m 2/0 V.A. Dum D., 7 men attached to D.83, 1 Officer and 2 men to D.3, 2 men D. 82	
	26.10.17		do	do
	27.10.17		do	do
	28.10.17		do	do
	29.10.17		7 men attached to D.83 Brigade, 1 Officer & 5 men attached D.82	2 Men attached to D.82 Bridges D.82
	30.10.17		1 man Returned from D.83 R.F.A.	
	31.10.17			1 man returned from D.82. F.A.

W. Good Capt.
for Officer Commanding
F. W. Z/18 J.H. S.P.

Army Form C. 2118

2/18 Jm Bg

WAR DIARY
or
INTELLIGENCE SUMMARY

(Erase heading not required.)

Instructions regarding War Diaries and Intelligence Summaries are contained in F. S. Regs., Part II. and the Staff Manual respectively. Title Pages will be prepared in manuscript.

Place	Date	Hour	Summary of Events and Information	Remarks and references to Appendices
Chelsea des Trou Tours	November 1917 1st		1 N.C.O. attached Zouave Dump A.N.R.D & 4 men attached D/83 Battery A.F.A 1 N.C.O and	
	2nd		2 men returned from B/82 Battery R.F.A.	
	3rd		1 N.C.O. attached Zouave Dump A.N.R.P. 1 N.C.O and 3 men attached D/83 Battery R.F.A	
	4th		1 N.C.O attached Zouave Dump A.N.R.P. 1 N.C.O and 2 men returned 2/183 Battery R.F.A.	
	5th		"	
	6th		1 man returned from 6/183 Battery R.F.A.	
	7th		1 men attached No 2 Section D.O.C for Signalling Course	
			1 N.C.O attached Zouave Dump A.N.R.P.1 N.C.O and 3 men attached 2/183 Battery R.F.A 1 man attached	
			No 2 Section D.a.C.	
	8th		"	
	9th		"	
	10th		"	
	11th		"	
	12th		"	
	13th		"	
	14th		"	
	15th		1 man attached to Salvaging Party	
	16th		"	
	17th		"	
	18th		"	
	19th		1 N.C.O. attached 5th Army School of Mortars	
	20th		"	
	21st		"	
	22nd		"	
	23rd		"	

WAR DIARY
or
INTELLIGENCE SUMMARY

Army Form C. 2118

Place	Date	Hour	Summary of Events and Information	Remarks and references to Appendices
Chateaudee Trois Tours	November 23rd		1 N.C.O. attached to new group A.K. +.O. 1 N.C.O. & men attached to D.S.3 Battery	
	24th		1 E.C.O. & men attached to 2 Section S.A.A.	
	25th		Party 1 N.C.O. attached to Army School of Instructors	
	26th		2 men attached to D/83. 1 N.C.O. returned from D/83.	
	27th		2 men attached to Salvaging Party	
	28th		"	
	29th		1 N.C.O. attached Salvaging Party	
	30th		4 men attached Salvaging Party	

Signed,
Officer Commanding
2/10 T.M.B.

Army Form C. 2118.

WAR DIARY
or
INTELLIGENCE SUMMARY.
(Erase heading not required.)

Z/18 T.M.B., R.A.

December 1917.

Ref. maps. { Staze trench 5ᴬ.
{ Sheet 28 N.W. Belgium 1/20,000

B.S. Weller Lt
OC Z/18 T.M.B. R.A.

Army Form C. 2118.

WAR DIARY
or
INTELLIGENCE SUMMARY.
(Erase heading not required.)

Z/18 TMB RA   December.

Place	Date	Hour	Summary of Events and Information	Remarks and references to Appendices
CHATEAU TROIS TOURS	1st		1 N.C.O. attached ZOUAVE DUMP. 4 men to D/183. 1 man to 5th Army T.M. school. 1 N.C.O & 8 men on Salvage.	
	2nd to 12th		1 N.C.O. & 8 men on Salvage. Remainder of battery in fatigues.	
CROMBEKE	13th		Battery moved by tram to Crombeke.	
	14th	9 Am	Gun cleaning, ammunition stores.	
	15th	9.30	Parade and inspection	
		9.45	Gun drill. 11 Am marching and Gas respirator drill. Kit inspection	
	16th	9.30	Parade & inspection	
	17th	9.30	Gun drill - marching drill, handling of arms, Gas respirator drill.	
	18th	9.30	Parade & inspection. Route to aid.	
	19th	9.30	Parade & inspection. Route march, Battery in Gas respirator	
	20th	9.30	Gun cleaning - route march.	
	21st	9.30	Route march. Gun inspection drill	
	22	9.30	Gun drill - handling of arms - Kit inspection. Inspection of billets by O.T.M.O	
	23	9.30	Parade & inspection.	
	24	9.30	Route march, marching drill. 2 men sent on leave.	
	25th	8	No parade 12.30 dinner to men	
	26	10 Am	Parade & inspection	
	27	9.10	Route march, Gas respirator drill, handling of arms	
	28	9.30	Route march gun drill, marching drill	
	29	9.30	Parade & inspection Gun cleaning	
	30	9.30	Parade inspection. Church parade for Presbyterians. Kit inspection. Inspection of billets by O.T.M.O	
	31	9.30	Parade inspection - fatigues.	

B. Alexander Lt.
OC Z/18 TMB RA

Army Form C. 2118

WAR DIARY
or
INTELLIGENCE SUMMARY
(Erase heading not required.)

January 1918.

Place	Date	Hour	Summary of Events and Information	Remarks and references to Appendices
Pioneer St	1st	-	Battery moved by lorries to forward area & took over billets of 87th Bde: French Mortar Bn at LARRY FARM.	
Larry Farm	2nd	-	General fatigues.	Camp B9614 Sheet 28. NW (Belgium)
"	3rd		"	
"	4th		"	
"	5th		"	
"	6th		"	
"	7th		"2" Battery T.M. Proceeded to Zevencote en route for 2nd Army T.M. School of Instruction.	
Vaux le Cousin	8th		Arrival Cousin.	
"	9th		Proceeded to School of Instruction at Vaux le Cousin.	
"	10th		At School of Instruction.	
"	11th		ditto	
"	12th		" " "	
"	13th		" " "	
"	14th		" " "	
"	15th		" " "	
"	16th		" " "	
"	17th		" " "	
"	18th		" " "	
"	19th		" " "	
Larry Farm	20th		Left School of Instruction for Larry Farm Camp (Elverdinghe) 9.30 A.M.	
"	21st		Arrived at Larry Camp.	
"	22nd		Battery Parade	
Stray Farm	to 31st		Salvage Party at Stray Farm.	

Chas A. [Springfield] 2/Lt R.F.A.
O/c 2/5 T.M Battery

31st Jan 1918.

www.ingramcontent.com/pod-product-compliance
Lightning Source LLC
Chambersburg PA
CBHW080923230426
43668CB00014B/2186